Lights in the Mist

Ronald L. Murphy, Jr.

Lights in the Mist

This edition published by Small Town Monsters Publishing, LLC in 2024

Author: Ronald L. Murphy, Jr.
Cover Artist: Easton Hawk

Table of Contents

Foreword

It was a bitterly cold night, and we were still about an hour away from where we were headed: Ron Murphy's house, hidden somewhere deep in the Chestnut Ridge. I'd driven through the area before, but I'd never taken the time to really explore it. We were driving from Pittsburgh to Latrobe, PA, to meet Ron for the first time. My girlfriend, Ariel Kline, was with me on this trip, the first weekend of scouting the Ridge for *Phantom Lights*, my first film with Small Town Monsters. Ariel, a Pittsburgh native, was my guide to the area, pointing out familiar landmarks and recounting local tales as we snaked through the dark, narrow roads.

We cranked up the heat another couple of degrees as we drove, joking about all the wild possibilities. Maybe Ron was some kind of serial killer or a vampire aristocrat, or maybe he was a mad scientist with a basement full of weird specimens. All this ridiculous stuff was a good way to keep our minds off the creeping cold outside and the shadows stretching out forever along the road. Of course, we were pretty sure Ron wasn't any of those things, but who knew? This was our first time meeting him, after all.

Ron was going to be a big part of the *Phantom Lights* project. He'd written *Lights In The Mist*, a book full of his research and personal experiences with these strange phenomena. The film and the book were meant to go hand in hand, a shared exploration of the unknown. That idea weighed on me a bit, though. What if I screwed up the film and made a great book like *Lights In The Mist* look bad by association? But first things first, we had to "survive" Ron and see how things went.

We pulled up in front of Ron's house, which sat right at the corner of Chestnut and Ridge. You couldn't ask for a more fitting name. The place was quiet in the falling snow, with a warm glow coming from the inside. We could see a family gathered around a dinner table, waiting for a guest. We checked the address on our phones, and, sure enough, this was Ron Murphy's place. We walked up to the door and knocked. Ron answered with a big smile, friendly right off the bat—exactly the kind of welcome you hope for when you're a little nervous. We were introduced to Ron's family and a large, chatty parakeet.

Ron took us into the dining room, where dinner was already set out: a spread of hearty, homemade dishes that felt like a balm after that long, cold drive. The room had that lived-in warmth that makes you feel at home right away. We settled in, and soon enough, the conversation was flowing. Ron's deep, rumbling laugh filled the space, and before long, we were swapping stories like we'd known each other forever.

As the meal went on, I started to really get who Ron was. He wasn't just a guy with a passing interest in weird stuff; he was deep into it. He talked about his love for folklore, cryptids, and the supernatural, sharing stories about his own encounters and research along the Ridge. Ariel and I were hooked, leaning in as he described strange lights darting across the hillsides and weird noises echoing through the woods at night. We tossed in our own thoughts on the strange and unknown between bites, cracking up over pop culture references, and bonding over our shared admiration for George A. Romero, Pittsburgh's own horror legend.

The conversation got deeper, from classic monster movies to the kinds of unexplained phenomena that seem to hang over places like Chestnut Ridge like a fog. Ron's eyes lit up when he started talking about the region's history, its deep ties to supernatural lore, and his theories on the Phantom Lights. You could tell he'd spent years putting together these stories, sightings, and local legends like some kind of strange puzzle. Ariel added her own thoughts, asking questions that got Ron talking even more, and soon the room was buzzing with that feeling of discovery.

By the time we'd cleared the plates, and the night had crept on, I could feel it—this was the beginning of something. A new chapter, yeah, but also a chance to dig into something deeper. This film, *Phantom Lights*, wasn't just going to be my debut with Small Town Monsters; it was a shot at capturing something that felt just out of reach, maybe even adding a little to the living, breathing story of this place. My worries about screwing things up started to fade away. After meeting Ron, I could see that our personalities would mesh well. His passion, his talent, his drive—it was all going to bring so much to the movie. It felt like we were already on the same page, working toward something that mattered.

And right there, surrounded by new friends and good conversation, I realized that whether we found anything out there or not, the journey itself would be worth it, just like the stories that filled Ron Murphy's dining room that night. *Lights In The Mist* and *Phantom Lights* weren't just separate projects; they were two parts of a bigger story, each giving the other weight. As we set out into the unknown of Chestnut Ridge and beyond, I felt a sense of calm. Whatever mysteries we were about to chase, I knew we'd be chasing them with good people and an open mind. And isn't that what looking for the unknown is all about? Being willing to wonder, to explore, and to share the story, wherever it takes you.

--Tyler Hall, Small Town Monsters, director of *Phantom Lights*

Introduction

Without the events that occurred in March of 2022, this book would not be written. While working on a film project concerning the phenomenon that is Bigfoot from the production team at *Small Town Monsters,* an investigative group of which I was a member encountered bizarre interactions with multiple earth lights. This is my attempt to wrap my head around what happened.

This book may seem like a work of fiction, strange and illogical in its structure and content, but I assure you these events actually happened to both me and fellow researchers and the historical events alluded to have been written in the annals of antiquity. This book is my attempt to uncover the origin of what have become known as earth lights, a seemingly sentient luminescence that may be biological in nature.

But in order to understand what happened to us in 2022, we have to first flashback nearly two decades. The account that follows is from the fall of 2004. It was not the first time I witnessed the earth lights, a radiant anomaly moving through the trees and weaving effortlessly within the landscape, but the events that I witnessed would transpire to become fuel for my subsequent nightmares and spark within me a quest to uncover the truth underlying what I witnessed. Many times, when I write on a subject, there is a catharsis involved, a sort of exorcism of my fears and trepidations. I am glad you, as the reader, are along for the ride.

I never sought out the phenomenon of earth lights. Of course, I had a working knowledge of their existence, but never really thought they were more than the proverbial "swamp gases" that was so easily an explanation for bizarre light anomalies. I consider myself a cryptozoologist. I'm educated in various concentrations and experienced with the workings of the natural world and in the ordered chaos within the human imagination. Now, this doesn't mean every time I venture out into the forest that I find evidence of the unexplained. Indeed, I am blessed with such a healthy share of skepticism that I often go out not actually believing in the query I seek! However, I am also knowledgeable enough to know that something is going on out there and has been for a very long time. In the ancient tales told by indigenous tongues and in the modern eyewitness accounts, there are uncanny commonalities to encounters with earth lights. As an academic researcher trained in the disciplines of anthropology and archaeology, most of my investigations I undertake are carried out in the wilderness of the library. As I sifted through ancient accounts, and as I reread eyewitness testimony of areas where such lights have been seen, I came to the conclusion that these lights were not merely sparks issued from the friction of tectonic plates or the occasion of the aurora borealis. No, something much more was at work within this phenomena.

In this particular investigation, I was not looking for earth lights but was examining the alleged sighting of a werewolf-like cryptid known as the Dogman. I ventured out around 9pm on a cold fall evening. The night was hideously dark. My flashlight scanned the leaves that were orange and red but still lingered on the trees. I was well off the beaten path, and any nuisance of light pollution was obscured by October's cloud cover. But this location was the rumored haunt of the Dogman, so I zippered my coat against the chill and set out down a path that twisted under a hill on which an abandoned cemetery glowered forlornly through the rustling tree limbs. Out here, on this sullen trail that carved its way through the autumn forest, I felt as if I were hopelessly adrift in a literal space between worlds.

As I swept the woods with my night vision camera, I was struck with the incredible feeling that I wasn't alone out here. I saw no animals through my eyepiece. No squirrel rustled through the leaves; no rabbit stirred the stillness. No. It was something else. Light anomalies seemed to follow me along the darkened path, nearly imperceptible in the fall night, but still there. I could plainly see the pinpoints of unmistakably living light flitter through my lens, little soft glows that darted and danced in the twisted undergrowth that lined the path, occasionally skipping out of the tangles and illuminating the trail. After my eyes adjusted to the night, I could see these illuminations without electronic aid. But I ventured onward, mesmerized, absent-mindedly following the lights that moved forward, leading me further afield. These will-o'-the-wisps were too hypnotic not to follow.

These luminescent orbs, subtlety changing colors as they moved onward, glowing in hues of blue and then green, then to white and an opaque yellow, guided me eventually to a long-abandoned railroad bridge that spanned a river that flowed lugubriously like a black ribbon in the valley below. The little lights that had accompanied me now left me as the woods halted at the bridge, seemingly to simply disconnect from my world before entering the open expanse of the bridge. I proceeded on until I made my way to the center of the bridge, where I felt oddly utterly exposed. The rather soothing electronic glow of the camcorder which I carried suddenly seemed to have its energy inexplicably drained, the battery light unexpectedly flicking on. Above me the sky that enclosed the world in its inky embrace seemed to spark with a static electricity, reminiscent of the electricity produced when you pull blankets from the bed. Was this St. Elmo's fire that sailors of old would tell tales? Something was happening to the world around me. Suddenly, a visceral urge shuddered my body. I knew instinctually that I had to get out of where I was. I must get back into those confining woods and make my way to my car, parked nearly a mile and a half away. At this point it was not a choice, it was an imperative drive to stay alive.

I turned. Behind me the trail disappeared as it was swallowed by the gaping void of the woods. But immediately as I turned, my eyes widened in trepidation. There, where the trail

3

plunged into the interminable abyss of the forest's gullet, a light of living intensity sparked to life, shimmering and sputtering like a contained Roman candle suspended in the air. I immediately called out, knowing rationally that there must be a person behind it. My mind worked with the information before me, struggling to process it intellectually. It must be a person. What else could it be? I glanced into my night vision camera's eyepiece. There was nothing there. The light was gone as quickly as it came. There was no person on the trail. Unnervingly, my battery icon in my camera was flashing an urgent SOS, begging to be recharged. It was as if the light that manifested before me used nearly all the remaining battery in my camera to power itself to life. Empirically that made no logical sense. However, cold and shivering from uneasiness, nothing else made better sense, and that gnawing instinct that sent a shiver of compulsion through me to run for my life was much more forceful now. I knew I must get out of these woods.

I quickly walked the bridge down towards where the light had ignited. Soon I made it to the tree line, shrouded by the overhanging branches that closed in on either side. I was alone. Utterly. The night was empty. Then an electricity shivered my body that instilled fear into me. I felt as if I were being watched. I also had the startling realization that I was being hunted. My quick walk became a trot until I found myself fumbling into the darkness at such a pace that my heartbeat pounded in my ears. My face stung as branches slapped my cheeks, my feet tripping over roots and through brambles as I veered from the trail in the absolute darkness. Soon I realized I would inevitably stumble and fall. Every primal instinct in my civilized brain screamed, insuring me that if I fell, I would be pounced upon. Something in the night was stalking me.

Then something inexplicable happened. Even telling you this now it seems rather difficult to believe, but I assure you of the veracity of the event. Off to my left, out in the woods and higher up, as if a person called out from the cemetery on the hill, I heard my name called. "Ron," it said. The voice was androgynous and undefinable. It was a quick gasp, yet stark in its immediacy. And it was an urgent call. Instantly, and hard to my left, something stirred in the twisted brush and in the littered leaves that covered the forest floor. On the other side of the trail, something was moving closer, stalking. I could hear its breath, the night air wet in its mouth. As the sticks snapped under its weight, I realized with unmitigated terror that I could "see" what was there. It was as if the synapses in my brain fired to produce an image of the creature that I knew was part of my collective unconsciousness. It was primal and bestial. It was the same menace that had pursued the human species since we first walked upright out of the African savannah. It was a Dogman. My brain constructed the creature, drawing it out of the memories locked within my DNA. It was huge, hulking. I could see each step it took was on paws that were more like hands. Its snout was lined with rows of needle-like teeth. Its nose smelled the air, pulling my scent out of the cacophony of odors that filled the woods. And those eyes. They were the eyes of a nightmare because they were the cause of nightmares since our genesis. The red eyes, narrowed with acuity. Seeking me out.

But I knew it was there. And it knew it as well. The little voice that called my name alerted me not only to the direction of the path that led to my car, but it also shook me to attention. I back peddled, looking through the viewfinder of my night vision camera toward where the creature stalked in the darkness. The battery, which had been dangerously low, now was reading that it still had over half its power. I quickly spun the camera around, finding the trail in the blackness of the night. Then I slowly followed the trail, keeping the night vision trained on where the Dogman lurked. I could hear it snarling, its breath wet and anxious.

But it never left its hiding place. It remained concealed in the thicket. Even when I had finally made it to my car and locked the doors before turning the key, I knew the creature was still crouched over in the forest, its eyes red, scanning the path, waiting for prey.

In reviewing the video evidence, I could see the little points of light were captured. So too was the light that ignited so brilliantly when I was out on the bridge. I realized that it was that light that drew me back into the woods. Why? Did the light have an intelligence? Did it know that there was a creature hunting in the woods? Other reports associated with the Dogman have occasionally reported strange lights. Is the Dogman interdimensional, and are the lights the visual evidence of portals opening? I'm not sure. But the lights did coincide with the appearance of this creature. And what about that voice that called my name? It did not appear on the film. That was my own little experience that cannot be shared. It was personal and poignant. The sounds of the creature prowling in the brush can be heard, but without that voice I am convinced I would have been pounced on from behind, blindsided by this predator. I feel that I would have been another missing person's case without this voice. But this time I made it out of the woods. I survived.

But most researchers would discount the lights, many not even recording it in the retelling of the encounter. Why? Because it doesn't make sense. A Dogman makes better sense to some investigators than intelligent lights emitted by the earth. What I experienced was lights that led me through the woods. My experience also suggests that these lights may also act as a kind of portal between two realities. Many earth light reports involve encounters in and around cemeteries, in conjunction with cryptid sightings, and, eerily, the accompaniment of strange voices whispering in the night.

In poring over accounts and historical documents, I realized that the experience I had was not unique. One of the reasons I research the paranormal is to lessen my fear of the unknown. But in the course of my work, rarely is that fear alleviated and more often it is magnified. In the world of witnessing strange phenomena of earth lights and events surrounding lights emanating from nature I quickly concluded I was not alone. For thousands of years, human beings have marveled at the strange phenomena called earth lights. To many diverse Native American cultures, these peculiar lights, which can appear as flickering flames of living light or intense balls of bioluminescence, marked the doorway to different realms. These earth lights were portals, and, in my account in this introduction to this book, my experience with earth lights suggests that indeed they can be seen as a conduit between two worlds. I assure you I was alone in the woods before I saw the light. I felt it instinctually. But when that light emanated, the fight or flight response overwhelmed me. Well, mostly the flight part of the response. As many Native American cultures believed, I feel that the light was the opening of another world into ours. Whatever was with me in the woods that night had come through the light. And that voice that I heard? Another intelligence in the environment? I am not sure. A ghost? No idea. But I felt as if the voice was part of an intelligence that sought to seek balance, that this light I had witnessed and whatever stepped through that portal somehow threw off the natural order of the area.

As I worked the events through my mind over the years, I do see many similarities with my story and other tales often related to cryptid research. One account involved an elderly woman who had set bags of garbage on her porch. This event took place in Western Pennsylvania, and it is common for folks in these parts to set bags of garbage on their porch days before the trucks come by to pick them up. But because the garbage is outside, critters tend to get into them. This particular evening, this woman heard a ruckus on her porch, and she believed raccoons were looking for a meal. She feared they were tearing open her bags. She picked up a shotgun, a common fixture in rural Appalachian homes, and opened the door only to meet a seven-foot-tall hair covered creature standing on her porch, looking at her with red eyes. Like any reasonable person would do who lives in rural Pennsylvania, she leveled her gun and fired point blank at the creature. But the creature did not succumb to the buckshot. No, the woman claimed this creature "disappeared" in a brilliant flash of light. Again, I must ask, is this a portal that is associated with these lights at least in these instances? It seems as such. A creature that should not exist in our world but seemingly does although no bodies have been found may allude to the fact that these creatures aren't wholly of our world and can use naturally occurring portals to leave our world and return to theirs. We must keep an open mind and objectively study all possibilities when we deal with any phenomena.

There are even more instances of earth lights at the infamous Skinwalker Ranch, also known as Sherman Ranch. It is a desert property of approximately 512 acres located southeast of Ballard, Utah, that is reputed to be the site of paranormal and UFO-related activities. Its name is taken from the skin-walker of Navajo legend, often perceived to be the monstrous manifestation by vengeful shamans.

The ranch, located in west Uintah County bordering the Uintah and Ouray Indian Reservation, was popularly dubbed the UFO ranch due to its ostensible 50-year history of odd events said to have taken place there. Researchers have investigated evidence of close to 100 incidents that include vanishing and mutilated cattle, sightings of unidentified orbs, large animals with piercing red eyes that they say were unscathed when struck by bullets, and invisible objects emitting destructive magnetic fields. Again, we see these earth orbs in a much larger context involving multiple paranormal phenomena.

The quest of this book, my friends, is to identify instances of these lights within the context of a historical backdrop. We will speculate on the nature of these lights and conjecture what meaning they have to us. We will seek to unravel this paranormal conundrum by removing one layer of this problematic preternatural onion at a time to seek out the cause and nature of what we call earth lights.

Shall we begin?

Transcendence—Where it All Began

I have always been fascinated by bizarre manifestations in the natural world. As a child I awaited school book fairs so I could get the latest copy of the Guinness Book of World Records. I would hurriedly rush to the contents that contained the natural wonders. Of course, the monumental records of the natural world never changed from year to year, but just seeing the highest and lowest temperatures recorded or the deepest part of our oceans led me to imagine even more outlandish possibilities. I wondered what still might remain in our world that was yet to be discovered. To this day, earth and her mysteries still captivate and inspire me. One such phenomena that drives my current research is surely the earth lights.

Earth lights, however, are something quite new to me and I wrote this book to inquire into what I have witnessed on numerous occasions. Although startling to encounter, the lights I experienced seem altogether wholly natural and part of this world that we live in. With that being said, I am not going to conclude this book with such a trite observation and flippant response. No, we necessarily need to delve deeper down this luminescent rabbit hole and see where it takes us.

As an historian by education, I adhere strictly to the notion that history does not exist in a vacuum. If we are witnessing earth lights now, then, if they do indeed exist, then they must have been noticed in the ancient past. There must be a precedent for this phenomenon. In short, there is tantalizing evidence that emerges initially from prehistory. This observation requires a healthy dose of speculation and conjecture, but I believe we can infer from what evidence we do have that ancient man not only was aware of earth lights but possibly even had an intimate understanding of what they were. It is in the recesses of our collective past that we will begin, in a world when we had not yet attained dominance over the land, when we were simply another shivering species subjected to the elements. It is within these conditions, when we were intrinsically connected to the earth, that these luminescent emanations impacted who we are as a species.

Earth lights are a rarely reported and often unappreciated anomalous light phenomenon, mistaken throughout history as dragons breathing fire, UFOs hovering over cornfields, and the naturally occurring anomaly known as ball lightning before being recognized as a separate category of the paranormal in and of itself. One leading theory is that these lights are produced by tectonic strain in minor fault lines, so that they are literally generated by the Earth. That may indeed be the source in many cases, but this explanation does not account for many of my encounters. So, there must be something else afoot. My thesis for this book is that earth lights are sentient and part of the tapestry of the living consciousness of the Earth itself.

I should get it out of the way and admit to you, the reader, who just began studying this book, that I am a firm adherent to the Gaia Theory. This theory states that our planet is truly Mother Nature, and it cares for us as much as we care for it in a symbiotic relationship based upon many principles of the norms of reciprocity. Before you toss the book over your shoulder in befuddled incredulity, let me explain this theory a bit more scientifically than just coming at you sounding like a fervent evangelist pontificating his personal New Age faith. The Gaia hypothesis, also known as the Gaia theory, Gaia paradigm, or the Gaia principle, proposes that living organisms interact with their inorganic surroundings on Earth to form a synergistic and self-regulating, complex system that helps to maintain and perpetuate the conditions for life on the planet.

The hypothesis was formulated by the very real chemist James Lovelock and co-developed by the acclaimed microbiologist Lynn Margulis in the 1970s. Sometimes you must name-drop to give a theory that sounds outlandish a tinge of credibility.

Lovelock named the idea after Gaia, the primordial goddess who was the personification of the Earth itself in Greek mythology. The suggestion that the theory should be called "the Gaia hypothesis" came from Lovelock's colleague, William Golding. So, my little belief doesn't so much sound like a fairytale anymore, does it? In fact, many intelligent men and women accept this idea, going as far as in the year 2006, when the Geological Society of London awarded Lovelock the prized Wollaston Medal in part for his work on the Gaia hypothesis. Various topics related to this hypothesis include how the biosphere and the evolution of organisms affect the stability of global temperature, salinity of seawater, atmospheric oxygen levels, the maintenance of a hydrosphere of liquid water and other environmental variables that affect the habitability of Earth. My main point of interest is the conscious nature of our planet and how this planet manifests its sentient nature to us. In one such way, I believe these earth lights have a role in this revelation.

Indeed, there are revelations around the world in the form of these lights. In America, these lights have been quaintly called "spook lights" or "ghost lights" since at least the 1950s, deriving from the assumption that these lights originate in the world of spirits. This belief, of course, harkens back to Old World traditions that were rooted in these same beliefs. These lights appear in many colors, various shapes, and sizes, though the basketball-sized spherical orange type seems most commonly reported by eyewitnesses. Most sightings occur at night when some of these lights can be seen from miles around. They're reported to be able to move against the wind and even reach extraordinary speeds. They seem to be of terrestrial origin but often times transcend the physics of gravity and become airborne. Earth lights simply do not abide by any hard and fast rules. They are a mystery to us in the modern world and, in our ancient past, must have been viewed as preternatural visitations. These earth lights would have certainly been known by the shaman and it is with the shaman that we shall begin our study.

The culture of the diverse groups of people who make up the aboriginal Australian people is one of the oldest on earth. A 2017 paper in *Nature* evaluated artifacts in the Australian region of Kakadu and concluded "Human occupation began around 65,000 years ago." This predates the cave paintings in France by at least 50,000 years! Yet even in this faint period in human development, beliefs come into focus as we study and deconstruct the traditions and beliefs of these people today. One of the most fascinating aspects of their cosmology is the notion of Dreamtime or the Dreaming.

The Dreaming is the world dawn of the Aboriginal, the beginning of everything. It has a beginning but has no foreseeable end. In this Dreamtime, the natural environment was shaped by the actions of mythic beings. These mythic beings of the Dreaming are eternal. In Aboriginal belief, they are spiritually as much alive today as they ever were. The places where the mythic beings performed some action or were metamorphosed into something else became sacred. I believe, if we connect the dots, we can see a relationship between the Dreamtime and a phenomenon known as the Min Min lights.

The Min Min is a light phenomenon that has often been reported in outback Australia. Stories about the lights can be found in several Aboriginal Australian cultures predating the European colonization of Australia in 1788 and have since become part of wider Australian folklore. Some Indigenous Australians hold that the number of sightings has increased in conjunction with the ingression of Europeans into the outback. In this belief, the old ways are revealing themselves to the present.

The Min Min lights are often seen as benign yet frightening and unknowable to those outsiders who experience them. Accounts of the light appearances vary, though they are most commonly described as being fuzzy, disc-shaped lights that appear to hover just above the horizon. They are often described as being white, though some accounts describe them as changing color from white to red to green and back again. Some accounts describe them as being dim, while other witnesses describe them as being bright enough to illuminate the ground under them and to cause nearby objects to cast clearly defined shadows. According to colonial folklore, the lights sometimes follow or approach people and disappear when fired upon, sometimes very rapidly, only to reappear later. It has also been said that anyone who chases the lights and catches them will never return to tell the tale of the encounter. Some modern-day witnesses to the Min Min luminescence describe the light as appearing to approach them several times before retreating. Others report that the lights were able to keep pace with them when they were in a moving motor vehicle. But is this tale unique? Can we find hints of earth lights in other cultures outside of Australia? To answer this query, we must enter the belief systems of other cultures. Our trek must necessarily begin with the shaman.

Archaeological findings have suggested that shamanism was practiced as early as 30,000 years ago. We, as humans, have been in our current anatomical and intellectual state for at least 200,000 years according to scientific consensus. In my opinion, the shaman stretches back at least that far in our lineage, and in other hominid forms, such as the Neanderthal, the practice of shamanism may extend much deeper into our evolutionary past.

Shamans were the embryotic priests in our human tradition, those who were set apart to be a conduit between the human world and that of the spiritual. Again, we see this idea reiterated in the worldview of the Australian Aboriginal, that we are part of and not separate from this world. The first burial uncovered with grave goods interred with the body dates to over 100,000 years ago. The goods placed with the deceased included flowers and various herbs, as well as parts of animals, such as feathers and teeth. In death, the human body was placed in the womb of the world that gave life and took that life away. The human form was united with the creatures which shared this life with the person who died. Keep in mind, animism was the only true dogma at this stage of our development, the belief that all of nature was imbued with a sentient spirit. Indeed, it can be said that all of nature was believed to be permeated with a governing, animating spirit. This term, "animism," is derived from the Latin word "anima," meaning an inherent life or spirit. Animism is the belief that everything in the natural world, all its myriad creatures, the inanimate rocks, trees, lakes and rivers, even geographical places, and weather, all possess a distinct spiritual essence. This essence also bound the world together, making us part of the natural world and not separate from it. The entirety of reality was animated and alive. This spirit possessed world interacted with us and communion with it was not only possible but essential. Everything around us was spiritual and supernatural. Animism encompasses the beliefs that all material phenomena have agency and that there exists no obvious distinction between the spiritual and physical world. Thus, in this animistic world view, we human beings are essentially regarded as equal with other animals, plants, and natural forces. We were necessarily tuned into the harmonious vibrations of the Universe. Our species' narcissism did not wholly develop until fortified towns were established, separating us from the natural world. But in the Paleolithic, we were just a part of the environment, helplessly at its mercy. Spirits existed in the Cro-Magnon imagination and worldview. Before the concept of good or evil, the spirit world would have been viewed as beneficial or malevolent. Before organized religion, the Divine was to be found in the world around us. We were not separate from that world but intrinsically linked to it; we depended on every aspect of nature for survival. In this intimate relationship, earth lights had to be accepted as sentient and possibly even communed with by the shaman. Without a written record this is purely speculation, but we must conjecture that earth lights, through the lens of animism, had to be considered entities within this world of ours.

While the paleolithic shaman left behind no record, in the subcontinent of India, the yoga certainly left behind hints of nearly extinct traditions and beliefs. The word "yoga" actually translates

14

closely to the English word meaning "union," revealing to us in its etymology that the yoga was, like the shaman, able to commune and go between worlds. It is as if the shaman in cultures around the world had not only knowledge of but access to what we would define as the portal. They were believed to literally go between worlds, to leave this world behind and enter another plane of existence. In that "other world" they would often return with knowledge of a healing medicine, information concerning the weather, or the best times to hunt. It is as if they entered a realm and had a revelation. As I have said, this is not an isolated belief but a worldwide understanding of the shaman and his or her abilities.

The first scientific evidence for the practice of Yoga was found in the *Vedas* which may be a tradition older than 10,000 years. However, many scholars assume that this tradition is much older than can be proven today. Shamanism, as well as Yoga, served our ancestors as a method to reconnect to the primordial soul and as a technique to experience the flow of existence. Shamanic traditions developed independently of each other all over the world. Yoga originated in India and was then spread all over the world.

Yoga and shamanism share the same view on our existence. Both traditions speak of the all-pervading energy. In Sanskrit this energy is known as the *prana*. Could these earth lights be identified by early man as a physical manifestation of this idea of *prana*? Yoga and shamanism teach us that there is no duality. Everything is connected and made of the same energy. Both traditions show us the way to merging with the primal soul.

Shamanic ceremonies were believed to be held around a ritual fire. The fire helps to transform energies and serves as a mediator between the material and the subtle world. The fire also plays a special role in Yoga. There are fire ceremonies, called *Havan*, to mediate between earth and heaven. The body's own fire, the *Agni*, is kindled through physical exercises and the right food. If the *Agni* is too weak, we become ill. Because in these worldviews everything is linked, are earth lights the manifestation of the *prana* in nature? Are the earth lights the *Agni* of the world in the concept of the theory of Gaia? Does the fire imitate the lights seen coming from the earth itself and we, in imitation, long for that cosmic union? I think we may be on to something here. If earth lights exist, and they undoubtedly do, and cultures have experienced them since we became anatomically modern humans, do they play a role in who we are? Let's dig a bit deeper.

Both shamanism and Yoga traditions ask supernatural forces for help. Thus, in shamanism, the power animal or a spiritual teacher is asked for advice. In Yoga, one seeks help from a guru, someone who metaphorically brings light into the darkness. Hinduism is not a polytheism. Hindus believe in one great energy, or a universal soul, termed the *Atma*. The different aspects of this soul are only represented by different deities which are all a part of the One. The *Atma* is the enlivening force, the Divine spark that is in everything. The goal in shamanism is usually to direct spirits or spiritual energies into the physical world for the purpose of healing, divination, or to aid human beings in some other way. The fire element serves this end because fire is symbolic of ritual purification and death. As earth lights originate from the ground, and bodies are buried in the ground, does the ritual fire attempt to conjure the earth light into some sort of sacred union with the living and the dead? Could this be why many ancient burial places around the world are very near the areas where earth lights are witnessed? Could these lights have been considered even protectors and these places held sacred? The element of fire is part of a chain of matter, of which the earth, water, air, and spirit are linked. We are made up of these elements in this worldview. But this Divine fire, this natural illumination, can transcend into super consciousness. Now we have left the world of science behind and find ourselves wading into the crashing surf of metaphysics.

Metaphysics is the only philosophy capable of inquiring beyond physical and human science. Traditionally, the word metaphysics comes to us from ancient Greece, where it was a combination of two words – *Meta*, meaning "over and beyond," and *phusika*, "natural things." Thus, the combination means something that exists outside of our preconceived governing rules of how things interact. When we study earth lights closely, they make no rational sense. It is in metaphysics, however, that this unifying fire becomes clear.

This imbued fire, this cosmic soul of enlightenment, symbolizes cleansing and purification, but it is more than just an emblem. Material fire is the symbol, and the fire of Spirit is the reality. The whole universe is alive with a divine, living, spiritual energy that consumes all the rubbish of physical sense and materiality.

But fire is not reserved for ancient animistic rituals; in fact, the notion of fire persists with us to the present day! The fire of God is the Word of God in action. It burns away the blindness of sinful consciousness and reveals the Christ. Spiritual fire is also illustrated in tongues of flame which is the icon for the illumination of thought in demonstration of God's Spirit's presence and power.

This image depicts the descent of the Holy Spirit during Pentecost. Before the Spirit manifested in lambent flame, there was the sound of a mighty wind. This Spirit derived from the natural world and revealed itself as an element of fire which has been held sacred since we have been humans.

Since time immemorial, paganism and esoteric philosophy have sustained the existence of elemental beings that coexist with us on astral planes or in a dimensional superposition –– these are only perceptible to some people, generally children, shamans or the initiated. If earth lights are sentient, can they be living entities? Can an element have a consciousness? We have, for the most part, left animism in the archaic philosophies of the past. But some great thinkers firmly believed that nature had an intelligence embroidered within it.

Elementals were an important aspect of the work of a gentleman named Paracelsus. To meet him, we have to swing by Germany in the mid-1500s. Paracelsus, born Theophrastus von Hohenheim in 1493, a year after Columbus' first voyage to what would become the New World, was a Swiss physician, alchemist, and astrologer of the period we now call the German Renaissance. He was a pioneer in several aspects of the "medical revolution" of the Renaissance, emphasizing the value of observation in combination with received wisdom. He is credited as the "father of toxicology." Paracelsianism is the early modern medical movement inspired by the study of his works.

Paracelsus stated natural science and chemistry were the groundwork of medicine. This guy is no joke; he actually gave the mineral zinc its name. Paracelsus used chemicals and minerals in the formation of what would be the medical field. Sickness and health relied on harmony of human and nature. He believed the entirety of the Universe was one coherent organization. He maintained that mental illness was a disease. And he also believed in elementals.

These natural intelligences, these entities of nature, became more categorized within the imagination of Paracelsus, becoming something known as an elemental. An elemental was not a term coined by Paracelsus, but rather an explanation for the unseen forces at work in the natural world. By this period in history, the elemental was of fundamental importance in occult and alchemical works. In his important 16th-century alchemical work *Liber de Nymphis, sylphis, pygmaeis et salamandris et de caeteris spiritibus*, Paracelsus identified these unseen, intelligent beings as belonging to one of the four elements. He wrote the book to "describe the creatures that are outside the cognizance of the light of nature, how they are to be understood, what marvelous works God has created." His paradigm for this was that each archetypal being was in control of one of each of the four elements. The gnome was the intelligence, the spirit of earth. The undine was a being of water. Sylphs were the entities of the air. Salamanders were the beings of fire. These correspond, of course, to the Classical elements of antiquity which were earth, water, air and fire.

This concept of these elementals seems to have been conceived by Paracelsus in the 16th century, though he did not in fact use the term "elemental" or a German equivalent. Paracelsus regarded them not so much as spirits but as beings between creatures and spirits, generally being invisible to mankind but having physical and commonly humanoid bodies.

To commentate on the antiquity of these beliefs from which Paracelsus drew, we must first look at one other appellation of the elementals he referred to as the sprite. The word "sprite" is derived from the Latin *spiritus* from where we obtain the root for spirit. Variations on the term include "spright," the origin of the adjective "sprightly," meaning spirited or lively.

In Paracelsus' paradigm, these sprites are mostly harmless unless threatened. Paracelsus describes these elementals

> "as the invisible, spiritual counterparts of visible Nature...many resembling human beings in shape, and inhabiting worlds of their own, unknown to man because his undeveloped senses were incapable of functioning beyond the limitations of the grosser elements."

In other words, our senses and perceptions are bound to this world because we are of this world. But unequivocally, this great Renaissance thinker believed in these elemental sprites even though they could not be readily seen. The world was, after all, permeated by spirits of nature.

These humanoid, etheric beings are the fundamental aspects of nature, the building blocks of reality. This system prevailed in the Classical period, as evidenced in Greco-Roman art, and earth, wind, water, fire, and air had a personification, once known as gods and goddesses, that would later be known as an elemental. This elemental world is the frame on which the goblin universe was built. This belief was highly influential even in the Middle Ages. Even the plants of the earth had attending sprites, developed more systematically and Christianized into the Doctrine of Signatures in the Middle Ages.

Although Paracelsus uses these Classical preexisting foundations rooted in Greek and Latin thought to name these elementals, he did this to expand on his own philosophical system and add credence to it by commenting on Classic references, grounding it firmly in established doctrine. His role as an alchemist insisted that he delve into the past to find the necessary answers to address the future. Alchemy, after all, is a philosophical and prescientific tradition that was practiced throughout the ancient world in varying degrees that aimed to purify and protect certain objects. Common aims were chrysopoeia or more widely known as the transmutation of base metals, such as lead, into noble ones, such as gold. Alchemists also sought to create an elixir of immortality. In their role as a precursor to the scientific approach used within medicine, alchemists endeavored to create a panacea, a medicine that would have the ability to cure any disease.

In 1566, Paracelsus wrote to "describe the creatures that are outside the cognizance of the light of nature, how they are to be understood, and what marvelous works God has created." In these works, Paracelsus discusses various elemental attributes and delves into these beings' interactions with our physical world.

These elementals were necessary components of the vibrational tuning of the universe. They controlled the natural powers in a sort of ordained way, affecting the desired effect prescribed by God within His creation.

Paracelsus suggested that the salamander was the elemental of fire, which has had substantial influence on the role of salamanders in the occult. Paracelsus, contrary to the prevalent view of the time, considered them to be not devils but similar to humans, only lacking souls. Paracelsus also believed in the element of ether, a somewhat psychic substance that transcends terrestrial and physical evolution. Luminiferous ether, meaning light-bearing, was the postulated medium for the propagation of light through the Universe.

This classification of elemental beings can be taken literally by some, in the sense that an abundant number of legends exist that depict encounters with elemental beings that are usually intrinsically related to Mother Earth or the Mother Goddess, almost as guardians or secret holders.

Salamanders, fire manifestations, are the expression of will, power, intensity, and ardor, both spiritual and erotic. Their incendiary nature can make them volatile and dangerous for those who interact with them.

Whether we only see these beings as symbols of the structure of nature or as subtle beings with which we can form specific relations, this classification allows us to structure the different energies and patterns of nature. Each thing is the result of a sort of contest between the elements —balanced or unbalanced, the dance of the complements—and from each thing and each relationship we can obtain fire, water, earth, and air, as needed. This understanding brings us closer to a vision of nature as a complex entity that expresses itself in different forms but that keeps an order and a secret language known only to itself.

And here we come full circle. The Aboriginal people of Australia also saw intelligences within the elements of this world. They were intrinsically connected to the land and understood nature on an intimate level. We hike and camp and pretend we have a connection with nature, but to be connected to the point that the earth's heartbeat is your heartbeat is unknown in the Western World and has been for about 3,000 years. The Australians even had a name for these elemental entities: the Wandjina.

Dreamtime is a term devised by early anthropologists to refer to a religio-cultural worldview attributed to Australian Aboriginal beliefs. The Dreaming is used to represent Aboriginal concepts of "time out of time," or "everywhen," during which the land was inhabited by ancestral figures, often of heroic proportions or with supernatural abilities. These figures were often distinct from "gods" as they did not control the material world and were not worshipped, but only revered. The Dreamtime is the eternal, uncreated world outside of our physical world. Both worlds do indeed merge into one another, but the Dreamtime is still seen as a separate dimension. It is my contention that the Dreamtime of the Aboriginal Australians was the same dimension contained in the concept of the faerie realm of the Europeans. For the Aborigines, the Dreamtime was inhabited by beings very similar to the Western notion of the faerie. This being was known as the Wandjina.

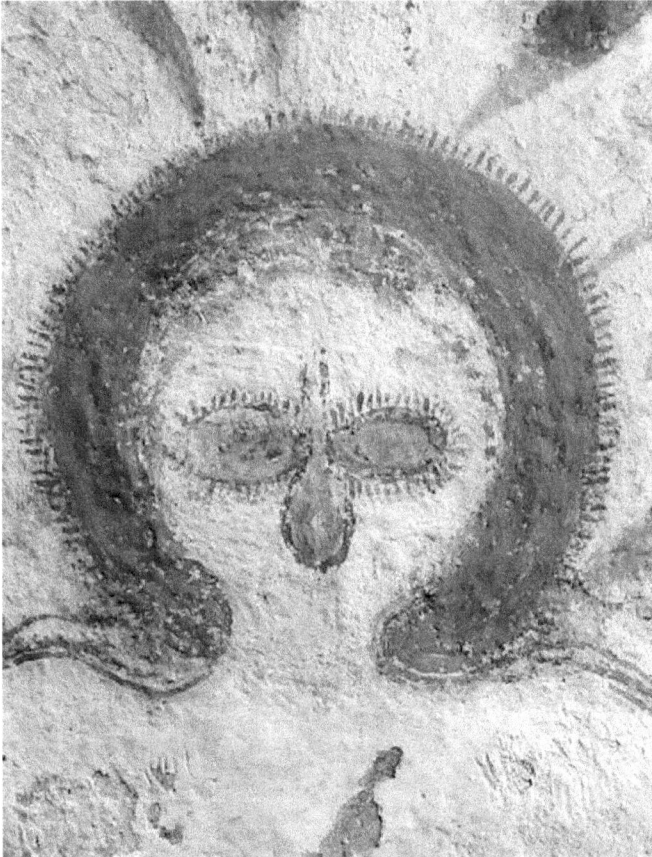

An ancient painting of a Wandjina, possibly 4,000 years old. Notice the energetic halo that forms a glowing aura around this entity. Did the artist intend to render the figure as glowing to the viewer? Even the eyes seem to emanate an energy.

The Wandjina are nature spirits from Australian Aboriginal mythology that are depicted prominently in rock art in Australia. Some of the artwork in the Kimberley region of western Australia dates back approximately 4,000 years ago. Dreamtime stories say the Wandjina created the landscape and its inhabitants and continue to have influence over both. When the spirits found the place they would die, they painted their images on cave walls and entered a nearby waterhole. These paintings were then refreshed by Aboriginal people as a method of regenerating the cosmic life force. We see this connection with the world of nature and the spirit world entwined in this particular being.

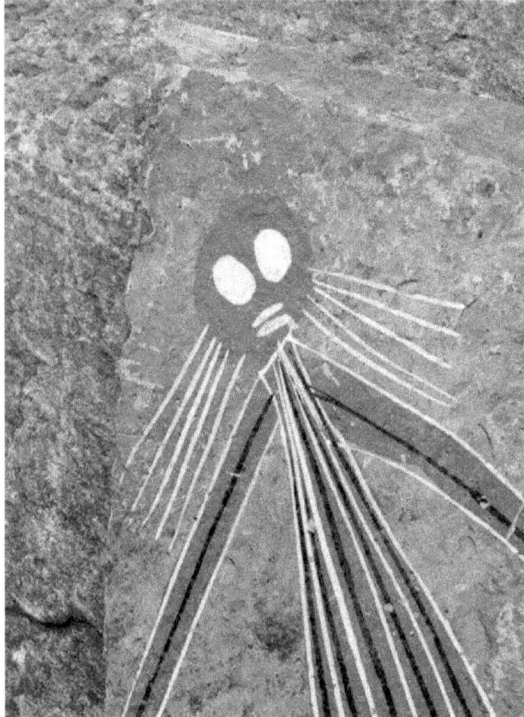

A depiction of the entity known as the Mimis created as rock art. Notice the lines that seem to suggest the sense of light cast from the body. This creature is said to live in the space between spaces. It is also known to live among the cracks in the rocks. Could this be a personification of an element or a depiction of an elemental?

But this was not the only being inhabiting the Dreamtime. The Mimis are earth-based beings in the folklore of the Indigenous Australians of northern Australia. They are described as having extremely thin and elongated bodies with the ability to fly. The Australian Museum in Sydney, in its web article entitled *Indigenous Australia Spirituality* describes them thusly: "The Mimi are tall, thin beings that live in the rocky escarpment of northern

Australia as spirits." Live in a rocky escarpment? This area of Australia is known for the appearance of earth lights. This entity, the Mimis, is supposed to actually live in and among the rocks? This may not just be a folksy explanation for the earth lights, an archaic personification of a mystery light seen by the ancients, but the actual source of the light itself!

Many people have suggested that the Wandjina specifically and to some extent the Mimis represented contact with an extraterrestrial race. Indeed, looking at those haunting faces of the Wandjina, it does seem as if we are dealing with something from out of this world. But why do we feel this? Well, for one thing, we come from a technologically advanced race, and we are assigning modern meanings to ancient symbols. What if we take this being at face value? What if what we have depicted in Australia was some of the last images of members of the entities that are the intelligences within the elements? What if communion with the elemental world was once an accepted part of the human existence, and now, when such encounters occur, we call them close encounters with aliens or hauntings rather than something fundamentally natural? As we go forward in this book, I will look from many different perspectives in an attempt to get a clearer view of what we call earth lights. But we must always keep in mind that we may indeed be dealing with a true natural entity.

I must say I am quite intrigued by the idea, the philosophy of the *prana*. To reiterate, within the tradition of yoga, inherent in Indian medicine and evident in Indian martial arts, the concept of *prana* is the breath, the sustaining life force, the vital principle that permeates reality on all levels including inanimate objects. In Hindu literature, *prana* is sometimes described as originating from the Sun and connecting and uniting the elements. The fire element, in many diverse cultures, is seen as enlightenment. The ancient religion of Zoroastrianism, derived from Iranian culture, is actually one of the world's oldest organized faiths. This religion undoubtedly came out of the belief of animism and developed into an organized dogma. Within this Zoroastrian worldview we see that fire is considered a medium through which spiritual insight and wisdom are gained. *Atar* is the Zoroastrian concept of holy fire, sometimes described in abstract terms as burning and unburning fire or visible and invisible fire. We must make no mistake about it, but as we read in the book of Exodus, the Judaic God certainly came out of a similar regional tradition in that He appears as fire consuming a bush that is, well, unburning. I think we in the Western world have so disassociated ourselves from the natural world that we lost the universal element that enlivens all religions. An integral part of that element is, in short, the elements themselves. We have driven out nature and replaced it with stained glass.

This idea of living fire is also expressed in the development of an Arabic religion that developed into what is Islam. The elemental within the Muslim worldview is a supernatural being known as the jinn. I must point out that there is the Islamic belief that these jinn were spirits of the elements, created thousands of years before our world. They were created by God out of the primordial fire that was part of the chaos before God established order. God says:

"Indeed We created man from dried clay of black smooth mud. And We created the Jinn before that from the smokeless flame of fire" (Quran 15:26-27)

We see that the nature beliefs in other societies trickle into the story of the jinn as well. As they are made of fire, angels were created from the element of light:

"The Angels were created from light and the Jinn from smokeless fire." (Sahih Muslim)

Because Islam derived from an Arabic belief system, it is readily apparent that the nature of a desert environment helped shape this religion. From a structuralist perspective, jinn are the binary opposite of angels. In a Judeo-Christian world, these jinn would be viewed as nature spirits of evil. The name jinn may have originally meant in a form of old Arabic something very near to "garden." There is a nature connotation readily apparent in this derivation, and if this is indeed the source then we are glancing back to an animistic conception of the jinn, long before organized religion corrupted the meaning and filtered the image of such an earth-based entity. Jinn are believed to be invisible to humans because we lack the appropriate sense organs to envision them. The prevailing notion is that the jinn live alongside us in an unseen world which merges with ours from time to time and which inhabitants of that world can sometimes seep over into our reality. It is readily apparent that the term genie is from the Latin *genius*, a guardian spirit of people and places in Roman religion. Again, no religion forms hermetically, there will always be outside influences in the development of theology. However Hans Wehr maintains in the *Dictionary of Modern Written Arabic*, the Arabic noun root means "to hide." Wehr also maintains that there are cognates in Arabic that means "possessed," "insane," and "embryo," indicating the nature of these entities. Something about it is incomplete and its interaction with humans is nefariously controlling. But let us focus a bit on the translation meaning "to hide."

The jinn, humans, and angels make up the three known sapient creations of God. According to Amira El-Zein, in the aptly titled chapter, "Jinn," from the informative *Medieval Islamic Civilization- An Encyclopedia,* the jinn, like human beings, can be good, evil, or neutrally benevolent and hence have free will like humans. The shaytan are jinn that are akin to demons in Christian tradition, but the jinn are not angels, and the Qur'an draws a clear distinction between the two separate creations. A jinn was thought to be a desert-dwelling, shapeshifting spirit that can assume the guise of an animal, especially a hyena. It lures unwary people into the desert wastes or abandoned places, the liminal regions, to prey upon them and devour them. Like encounters with the will-o'-the-wisp, in the English vernacular, which was said to resemble a flickering lamp and was rumored to recede if approached, drawing travelers from the safe paths, travelers needed to be on guard of a predatory jinn as well in the vast deserts of the Middle East.

Other tribes of these jinn were known to oppress mankind if they chose to do so. One of the powers of the jinn is that they can take on any physical form they like. Thus, they can appear as animals, trees and even humans. Thousands of people have reported seeing strange creatures all over the world, and the Muslim explanation maintains that it seems more plausible all these sightings of such cryptid creatures may have been jinns parading in different forms. Was the Dogman I felt stalking me actually a thoughtform from a jinn?

But the Arabic world also has other nature spirits inhabiting it, not just the jinn. Another ethereal entity is known as the hinn. The hinn are considered part of the "circle of time", belonging to a period preceding the creation of mankind. This is very reminiscent of the Australian conception of the Dreamtime, which is also inhabited by similar entities. In this Middle Eastern belief, therefore before humanity left its mark on the world's stage, the hinn and jinn roamed the earth. But elementally the hinn were separate from the jinn. Whereas the jinn were said to be created from smokeless fire, the hinn are believed to have their naissance from scorching flames.

Some adherents to the religious traditions believe that the hinn are extinct. Only the jinn remain in hiding. However, there are still whisperings that some hinn remain among us, occasionally shapeshifting into the guise of a dog. Or possibly a Dogman?

Throughout history man has always had a deep attraction for the supernatural and an awe when confronted by the unseen forces of nature. The Islamic world was no different. Even today, most Muslims readily accept the existence of spirits known as the jinn. These jinn straddle our world and another dimension where

28

angels tread. The existence of a world parallel to our own has always fascinated people. This world is commonly referred to as the spirit world, and almost every culture has some concept of this incorporeal realm. In the dogma of Islam, spirits are either the forces of good or the forces of evil.

There is a seemingly instinctual understanding that there is intelligence within fire and the flame, and as you will see as you make your way through this book many eyewitnesses of earth lights describe them as a true flame lambent yet intense in its manifestation. Considering this notion, I can make a connection with the iconography of the Middle Ages which first began to illustrate the revelation of the Holy Spirit as a flame alighting above a saint's head. This is the *prana*, the Divine spark, within us, illuminating us. This was even illustrated in Martin Scorsese's movie, *The Last Temptation of Christ,* in a scene where the character of Jesus is first tempted by the devil in the wilderness. Unlike the typical serpent that often represents evil, as depicted in the opening scene of Mel Gibson's *The Passion of the Christ*, Scorsese choses to depict the devil as an intelligent flame emanating from the earth itself, with the voice of ex-Genesis front man, Peter Gabriel. This visual idea may have come from John Milton. In literature, the will-o'-the-wisp sometimes has a metaphorical meaning, describing a hope or goal that leads one on but is impossible to reach, or something one finds sinister and confounding. In Book IX of John Milton's *Paradise Lost*, written in 1667, the author states in lines 631–642, that Satan is compared to a will-o'-the-wisp when he leads Eve to the Tree of Knowledge of good and evil:

> [As] a flame,
> Which oft, they say, some evil Spirit attends,
> Hovering and blazing with delusive light,
> Misleads the amazed night-wanderer from his way
> To bogs and mires, and oft through pond or pool;
> There swallowed up and lost, from succour far.

—9.631-642

Again, as I have pointed out previously, history does not exist in a vacuum and these ideas of living flame within our world transcends cultures, time, religion, and place. These lights are transcendent. The *prana* may be an Indian term, but it is applicable to Western thought as well. Is this what we are dealing with when we encounter these so-called earth lights? Are we experiencing a manifestation of Earth's *prana*, the unifying lifeforce, from within our world?

A Haunting of Orbs

Before I went down this proverbial rabbit hole and started to investigate, write, and lecture on the paranormal, I was an avid yet passive fan of all things that go bump in the night. I would watch all the ghost hunting shows. 20 years ago, the programs that concentrated on ghost investigations weren't so confrontational, focusing more on the history and less on the more fantastical. Now everything is demons because that is what people want and therefore this is what networks air. Indeed, two decades ago was a simpler time. The theme throughout these shows was that the evidence presented in the form of orbs. That was the proof that ghosts lingered in a certain area. An armchair researcher photographing a ghostly orb would be akin to an amateur golfer lucking into a hole-in-one. So, I took my family to Moundsville Penitentiary in Moundsville, West Virginia in the hope of proving myself a true investigator of ghostly activity. What better location to begin than a prison that witnessed many murders while operational?

I had in my arsenal a first-generation digital camera I bought at Walmart. It was clumsy and had terrible resolution with a screen not much larger than a postage stamp, but this was state of the art gear in 2003. As I made my way through the labyrinthine structure built to punish criminals, I found a little unassuming alcove. I quickly stepped into the recess and snapped a rapid succession of pictures. No longer having to drop off film and wait 4 days to have it developed, I could immediately scroll through the photos to see if I had captured any evidence. To my surprise, I did! A red orb showed up in several of the frames, seeming to undulate and move as it appeared differently in each picture, moving throughout space. I had captured a ghost! But did I?

You see, the reason Moundsville is known by that name is because directly across the street is an ancient earthen Indian mound called the Grave Creek Mound. This burial mound was created during what archaeologists refer to as the Woodland period, around 1000 BC to about 1 AD. The people who lived in the area during this time are among those groups classified as Mound Builders because mound building was a hallmark of their culture. This tumulus or burial mound was built in successive stages over a period of a hundred years. In the late 1800s, a hastily conducted excavation took place at the mound, without any true archaeological standards applied to what amounted to little more than a pillage of the site. At approximately 111 feet into the mound a burial chamber was discovered. The burial chamber was reported to have been a cuboid measuring 8 feet by 12 feet, aligned north-south and dug 7 to 8 feet into the natural ground surface. A lower tomb contained two burials, one on the eastern side and the other on the western. The western burial was found with approximately 650 beads of either shell or ivory. The second two tunnels were dug following the discovery of the lower vault, one vertical from the top into the mound and the second approximately halfway up on the northern face. These two shafts intersected at a second burial chamber, containing a single interment. Among the artifacts reported were 1700 ivory beads, 500 seashells, and five copper bracelets.

In other parts of the world, earth lights are often seen in and around places set aside for burial. My question is this—are these lights representative of the souls of the deceased or did the ancients decide to bury their dead in places where the earth lights were seen? In the shamanic tradition, this would be seen as a way for the bodies to once again be absorbed by the enlivening fire of nature, the body becoming one with the soul of the earth. Are we really chasing ghosts or do many things we associate with hauntings derive from the land itself?

For most of my life I have been involved in education in some capacity. Several years ago, I was teaching in a small elementary school. The principal found out from a newspaper article that I investigated local hauntings and asked if I would be interested in taking some teachers and staff out on a ghost hunt during the Halloween season. I must tell you I was not thrilled by the prospect of taking a group of middle-aged ladies into the woods looking for evidence of the afterlife. So, I told her that I would consider the possibility. Later that day a young teacher named Abby caught me in the hall and said, "I heard you were taking us out on a ghost hunt. Is that true?" I looked at her and smiled, answering, "Yes, it is." Hey, I am a hopeless romantic.

As it happened, we all gathered for a ghost hunt near an old cemetery the first day of November. It was cold but bearable, and the trees were heavily laden with leaves the color of precious gems. I pointed out some of the more notable people buried in the cemetery, one such grave honoring one of the few survivors of Custer's last stand at the Battle of Little Bighorn. I told the tales they wanted to hear, of phantom horses and spectral riders, of witches and of various other paranormal activities that would at least satisfy their craving for the themes of the investigations they watched on television. To end the evening, I decided I would lead them to the site of an abandoned train tunnel that was the location of a deadly train crash nearly 100 years ago. It was towards evening, with the sun setting in vibrant oranges and reds that painted the woods in a magical palette. As we came upon the tunnel, the sun was but a glimmer beyond the trees that palisaded along the western horizon.

I told the story of the train disaster a century before us, giving details of the boiler that exploded and the burns that one of the victims received that liquified his skin. I pointed out the loss of limbs and the terribly agonizing deaths that befell those unfortunate workers and passengers of the train. I spoke about the rumored ghost train, still witnessed to this day, its evocative whistle rumored to sound deep in the night.

Then I made my way to the tunnel like an actor strutting across the stage. The tunnel was barred off, but there was an opening in the grating. I informed those gathered for my tour that inside the ghosts still lingered, haunting the tunnel. Of course, I had no real knowledge concerning any paranormal activity involving this tunnel, but it was getting dark, it was spooky, and I was putting on a good show! Several eager young teachers squirmed through the breach in the grating and explored the tunnel, their flashlights feebly attempting to illuminate the abyssal depth and cavernous breadth of the chasm that yawned into complete and utter darkness, swallowing them entirely in its enclosure. I was taking pictures with a far superior digital camera than the one I employed at Moundsville, when suddenly I noticed a shiny, translucent orb rise out of the ground very near to where the women stood. It was as if it dripped out of the sandstone and shale but in reverse, defying gravity and falling upward. It seemed to have a mass to it and the roundness of the object undulated, elongating into an oval at times and returning to a circular shape in other instances. I checked the images captured digitally and discovered that this orb flitted through several photos. It was never stationary, but it moved about those gathered within the tunnel as if they were being inspected. I felt the immediate sense as if their intentions were being evaluated by this mysterious luminescence. I must state that these orbs could not be seen by the naked eye; they were only captured on the digital lens. The glow that was revealed in the lens could not be physically seen, the tunnel still very black. But I watched intently on the lens for minutes, even yelling out to the women what I was seeing through the camera.

They indicated that they indeed did feel sudden temperature changes and their skin was "prickly." Were their bodies reacting to some sort of localized electrical phenomenon? Then Abby said she had a sudden headache. To my astonishment, I could see through the camera Abby, the teacher who complained of the headache, did not have a face! Her body, wrapped in a black peacoat, was very visible, but her face was blotted out by this glowing orange light. When she walked, the anomaly stayed over her head, fogging her appearance. The light was there, that late Autumn orange-colored glow, but her face was blocked by it. It clung there for at least two minutes before it shot off and disappeared into rock that formed the rounded ceiling of the tunnel. I am an experienced investigator but having never been confronted by something such as this I felt it was better that we leave this area and go home. The women agreed and as I helped Abby, the one who had the orb fixated on her, wriggle through the hole in the gate, she said, "My headache is gone."

It was a two mile walk back to the car. Everyone who was giddy for this Halloween adventure was now quiet. Remember, not everyone saw the orb. I saw it and showed it to another person whose name was Raychelle. Only she and I bore witness visually to the object. But everyone in our group was affected in some way. Of course, it was getting late. Certainly, they were tired. But there was more to it. We all seemed physically and psychically drained. The walk seemed as if it were endless until more orbs appeared.

By this time the sun had vanished long before and above us Orion shone in the sky. Lacking any ambient light, the sky was as clear as a planetarium projection. This darkness made the earth lights at the crest of the hill we were climbing seem even more intense in their glow. A green and blue light, appearing as pinpoints but probably the size of golf balls, jumped sporadically across the path. They seemed to shoot out of the ground and leap over the trail then leap back to the other side. At this point everyone got a rush of adrenaline, and our walking pace became a run. Then as we drew very close to where the orbs bounded about, the lights blinked out as quickly as if someone turned off a switch. As soon as the lights vanished, the voices began.

The voices were feminine in tone and there were many of them, a cacophony that rose from the trees themselves, emanating from the forest off to our left. If a disembodied voice has the physicality to chase someone, that is exactly what was happening. We ran without turning around, up the trail, turning in a bend at the summit that led to our cars. Sometime between reaching that bend and arriving to our automobiles, the voices ceased. They may have quieted earlier but my heart was beating so fast and hard it was the only sound in my ear. I gasped for breath as many of our group jumped into their cars and locked their doors. Then I felt a hand on my shoulder.

I jumped and the pulse in my ear began to bang again. Startled, I quickly spun around. It was Raychelle, the other person who saw the orb through the lens. "Sorry to scare you," she said, breathlessly, "but my side started to burn when we heard the chanting." It was odd she regarded the voices as chanting; I only heard voices rising and joining. Thinking about it in retrospect, chanting probably comes closer to what we heard in the woods that night. "And look." Raychelle pushed back her heavy coat and pulled up her woolen sweater. She had three scratches etched into her skin. "That was the reason for the burning." They were inflicted when the orbs disappeared and the chanting commenced.

This incident blurred the line of traditional hauntings. It was as if many different paranormal elements came into play that evening. We were in that gray area where nothing was typical and there was no rational answer to what we experienced.

When dealing with so called hauntings, we truly do not know the actual nature of what we refer to as a ghost. All the events of that night could be explained in haunting terminology. An intelligent spirit within the tunnel. The residual disembodied voices embroidered into the landscape. The scratches of a possibly demonic entity. And of course, the requisite orbs. But a haunting was not the impression we had. Of course, all paranormal phenomena are objective, but although these events checked all the boxes when it comes to a haunting, no one in our group felt as if this was ghost related. It was somehow different. Unique. It seemed to be a warning, but it was problematic to decipher. I feel as if we were somehow gifted this encounter, but we were shown the capabilities of the lights as a warning to tread no deeper. That is what I took from it, nonetheless. At the time of this writing, these events are now some three years on. None of those who experienced the orbs work together nor does anyone talk about that night. I reached out to the participants of our little group from that night over social media and one of the teachers involved named Amy simply wrote back, "That is something I will never think about again." The other messages were left unread.

As I have stated, these lights are not witnessed only in western Pennsylvania. The reason I am undertaking writing this book is because these lights are ubiquitous and all cultures from around the world would recognize such a phenomenon. Many times, cultures will indeed categorize these manifestations as hauntings. *Aleya*, translated closely to something akin to a marsh ghost-light, is the name given to a strange light phenomenon occurring over the marshes as observed by Bengalis, especially the fishermen of Bangladesh and West Bengal. This marsh light is attributed to some kind of apparitions that confuse fishermen, causing them to get lost or to lose their bearings, and may even lead to drowning if one decided to follow them moving over the marshes. Local communities in the region believe that these strange hovering marsh lights are in fact ghost lights, being the ghosts of fisherman who died plying their trade. There is an ambivalent nature to these lights; sometimes these lights confuse the local fishermen, and sometimes they help them avoid dangers.

Similar assumptions that these lights are associated with ghosts is a prevalent cultural explanation in earth light folklore from around the world. *Chir batti*, translated as the "ghost light," is a strange dancing light phenomenon occurring on dark nights reported from the Banni grasslands, its seasonal marshy wetlands, and the adjoining desert of the marshy salt flats of the Rann of Kutch near the Indo-Pakistani border in what is known as the Kutch district, in the Gujarat State of India. Local villagers have been seeing these lights sometimes hovering, sometimes transforming into flying balls of light, since time immemorial. This is very curious indeed, as Yoga was formulated here and, connecting the dots, the idea of sentient lights begins to come into a bit clearer focus. I believe that the notion of the *pani* began with ancient observations of these lights and theories concerning their nature became part of the cultural religious doctrine of that area. These lights must have been perceived as the life breath of the world itself, the enlivening spirit that connects humanity to the natural world. This is the animus, the One Soul.

Similar phenomena are described in Japanese folklore, including the *Hitodama*, which translates as the "Human Soul," because the Japanese view the soul as a ball of energy capable of producing light! In fact, sometimes the human soul is referred to as "*Hi no Tama*," which means, tantalizingly enough, a "ball of flame." All these phenomena are described as balls of flame or light, at times associated with graveyards, but occurring across Japan in a wide variety of situations and locations. Kitsune, the mythical yokai demons, are also associated with what is called in the antiquated Western vernacular, the will-o'-the-wisp.

The will-o'-the-wisp is a European name alluding to a universal concept which is that the spirits of deceased humans glow. In Sweden, the will-o'-the-wisp represents the soul of an unbaptized person trying to lead travelers to water in the hope of being baptized. This emanation is sometimes referred to as spook lights for that reason. In our Halloween tradition, the candle in a pumpkin represents this sprite, this will-o'-the-wisp, this elemental spirit. Its name originates from the reported phenomenon of strange lights witnessed flickering over peat bogs, called will-o'-the-wisps or jack-o'-lanterns. Outside of Irish and other European traditions, other countries also have remarkably similar tales of their own versions of the will-o'-the-wisp lights.

In Argentina and Uruguay the will-o'-the-wisp phenomenon is known as *luz mala*, or the evil light, and is one of the most important myths in both countries' folklore. This phenomenon is quite feared and is mostly seen in rural areas. It consists of an extremely shiny ball of light floating a few inches above the ground. In Colombia, *La Candileja* is the will-o'-the-wisp ghost of a vicious grandmother who raised her grandchildren without morals, and as such they became thieves and murderers.

In the afterlife the grandmother's spirit was condemned to wander the world surrounded in flames.

In Trinidad and Tobago, a *Soucouyant* is a "fireball witch," that is, literally, a witch that takes on the form of a flame at night. This spirit is, like the other versions, evil in nature, a malevolent force in the world. The *Soucouyant* is believed to enter homes through any gap it can find, and therein drinks the blood of those inside.

Closer to home, there are strange spook lights, called by various regional names around Missouri and Oklahoma, such as the Hornet Spook Light, the Hollis Light, and the Joplin Spook Light, which is a ghost light reported to appear in a small area known locally as the "Devil's Promenade" on the border between southwestern Missouri and northeastern Oklahoma, west of the small town of Hornet, Missouri. Even though it is named after a small, unincorporated community in Missouri, the light is most commonly described as being visible from inside the Oklahoma border looking to the west. The spook light is usually described as a single ball of light or a tight grouping of lights that is said to appear in the area regularly, usually at night. Although the description of the light is similar to that of other visual phenomena witnessed throughout the world, the term "spook light", when standing alone, generally refers to this specific case. Numerous legends exist explaining the origin of the spook light, one of which involves the ghosts of two young Native American lovers looking for each other.

According to most accounts, these spook lights were known intimately by the Native Americans of that region and are rumored to have appeared continually since the late 19th century, although it was generally not well known to anyone but locals until after World War II. Some date the first encounters with the light back to the Trail of Tears in the 1830s. The first documented sighting is generally accepted to have occurred in 1881, although some report sightings as far back as 1866. The earliest published report dates to 1936 in the *Kansas City Star*. In 1946, the U.S. Army Corps of Engineers studied the Hornet Light, but could not find a cause for it. In their words, it was a "mysterious light of unknown origin."

Early residents settling the area reported seeing lights in the woods, over their land, or even in their yards. During the 1960s, a general store in Hornet gave out information about the light to sightseers. It even tried to turn a profit and opened a "Spook Light Museum" which was little more than a tourist snow job. Various establishments along the Missouri–Oklahoma state line have served a similar function but have since closed. During the 1960s and 1970s, the roads where the spook light usually appears were often packed with parked vehicles and people hoping to get a glimpse of the mysterious light.

Eyewitnesses say the best chances for spotting the light occur after dark when parked on Oklahoma East 50 Road, four miles south of the tri-state junction of Kansas, Missouri and Oklahoma in Ottawa County, Oklahoma, and looking to the west. It is said one must sit very silently. You must let the earth settle around you and then something from the earth itself seeks you out. The orb's color is inconsistent; some eyewitnesses reporting a greenish glow, while others describe it as orange, red, yellow, or even blue. It is almost always said to be in the shape of a ball, although some say it more closely resembles a camping lantern traveling a couple of feet off the ground.

In scouring newspaper reports, I was able to uncover some interesting first-person testimonies into the appearance of these spook lights. One witness outside of Louisville, Kentucky encountered an orb in his own backyard and interestingly enough reported that the light was a flame, and he did not just happen to see it. He reported that he was overcome by a creepy feeling which would not let go even after he was in bed. This feeling compelled the witness to get up out of bed and go to a hall window to look outside and when he did, he saw the flame "standing" about 10 feet from the window, hovering just off the ground. The witness stated it was like it was staring at him, letting him take a good look until he could comprehend that it was calling out to him. Again, as with my encounter recorded in the introduction to this book, we have the notion that these lights have a knowledge of their surroundings and those with whom they make contact. This reads like a report of a haunting, with the disembodied vocalizations and the orb of light, but indeed this was not an element of ghostly activity. Rather, it occupies that ambiguous gray area in the field of the paranormal. These lights produce confusing feelings and are very subjective. While many see these lights as "spook lights," this witness saw it as something environmental. He went on to say the light went out very quickly and popped up several feet away and continued this lighting and extinguishing pattern, but with increasing speed. The witness emphatically reiterated that the light that called out to him was indeed a flame, like a butane lighter, but slightly larger. He claims he was close enough to it that there was no mistaking it. He felt as if the light was a living entity within the environment itself.

A young woman had a similar experience. She also saw this light out her window and attempted to figure out the cause of what she was seeing. She had the tenacity to go outside and turn off all electrical outdoor lights. When she did, the flame lingered but a moment before extinguishing. It seemed as if the flame, in this instance, was observing her, hiding within the ambience of the artificial lights. As with my encounter that involved the schoolteachers, these lights seem to have the tendency to watch and evaluate a person. Evaluation requires intelligence. So, too, does communication. This may be the reason we call them spook lights. Without a rational explanation, what else could interact with people except, possibly, the disembodied soul of the deceased? A ghostly explanation makes sense when no other explanation will suffice. But earth lights aren't about making sense.

Realm of the Fae

This investigation occurred in 2013. It deliberately took place on the first day of summer. This is traditionally the time faeries wander about our world. Indeed, on this day, something very akin to faeries seemed to be wandering about our research group. Shortly before 9 pm, one sharp wood knock was heard emanating from a flat wooded stretch of land on the other side of the Conemaugh River in Westmoreland County in Pennsylvania. Within minutes, one deep howl was heard.

Suddenly from down the trail, a light emerged. It appeared to be the soft round glow of a flashlight, but as the light moved eastward, toward us, it suddenly vanished. One of the investigators said another of the other team members must be coming our way. He called out but no answer was made in reply. But now a light moved on, illuminating either side, peripheral on the trail. However, there was no source of light to cause this effect. It was as if the light causing the emanation around it was absorbed by the darkness itself. This strange effect of a ring of light without a source at its center continued toward us quite quickly before disappearing altogether just yards from us.

As we followed the trail, we entered the dark confines of the enveloping woods. The limbs so canopied the way that the sky was obscured completely by branches and leaves. On all sides of us were pinpoints of nearly LED intense white light. We assumed that they were fireflies, but upon further journeying down the trail, we concluded that although fireflies were indeed present, not a single light was one of the glowing insects! Indeed, the quality and luminosity of the brilliant lights illuminated the trail for us, moving with us. We allowed the light to lead the way, and it did until we came to the bridge on which the other team members were stationed. We stepped onto the bridge and as soon as we left the trail, the lights vanished as well.

We talked with the other team members to see if anyone did indeed venture up to meet us. They assured us that no one had. After collecting ourselves for nearly half an hour, we decided to return to our cars. As we walked back up the trail, we noticed that as soon as we left the bridge and walked the trail, entering the woods, the steady points of light rejoined us. This time they led the way, always several yards ahead of us, illuminating both sides of the trail.

The lights we witnessed this Midsummer seemed alive. They seemed to be orbs of bioluminescence that interacted with us, almost gifting us with its presence. These lights were impossibly difficult to categorize or label except for a strange occurrence in the woods. To me, it felt as if we witnessed the physical emanations of what is known as the will-o'-the-wisp.

In folklore and superstition, will-o'-the-wisp are typically attributed to not only ghosts, but to faeries or elemental spirits. In this context, we are not going to leave the subject of the will-o'-the-wisp, not just yet, but we are going to approach the phenomenon not from the angle of a ghostly manifestation but rather the correlation between the will-o'-the-wisp and the realm of the elemental.

In folklore, a will-o'-the-wisp is an atmospheric ghost light seen by travelers at night, especially over bogs, swamps, or marshes. The phenomenon is known in English folk belief by a variety of names, including jack-o'-lantern, friar's lantern, hinkypunk, and hobby lantern and is said to mislead travelers by resembling a flickering lamp or lantern. In literature, the will-o'-the-wisp metaphorically refers to a hope or goal that leads one on but is impossible to reach, or something one finds strange or sinister. In European folklore, many times these lights are believed to be spirits of the dead; other times the lights are believed to be the spirits of unbaptized or stillborn children, flitting between heaven and hell. However, faeries, or a variety of other supernatural beings which have their genesis in faerie lore, are seen to be the reason for the lights which attempt to lead travelers to their demise. In faerie lore it must be remembered that the dead are often associated with the fae and thus we have a mingling of different traditions and beliefs. But in examining earth lights more closely, it is odd that the dead keep recurring. When we discussed the yoga concept of *prana* and the Latin concept of the spirit, I truly believe we are connecting the dots a bit more and getting a clearer picture of what is causing the emanation of these lights. It is about the conception of the soul not just in humanity, but also in the very Earth itself.

Faeries have long been rumored to be keepers of great treasure or beings that are cognizant of where great wealth is stored. Consider the leprechaun and his pot of gold. In the legends found among such diverse groups as the Danes, Finns, Swedes, Estonians, Latvians, Lithuanians, and Irish people and amongst some other groups, it was believed that a will-o'-the-wisp also marked the location of a treasure deep in ground or water, which could be taken only when the fire, the earth light, was there. Again, we have the connection with the earth and sentient fire that manifests from the earth itself. In Finland and several other northern countries, it was believed that early autumn was the best time to search for will-o'-the-wisps and the treasures contained in the ground below where the earth lights appeared. We also see a connection with geographical areas that correspond to the presence of earth lights.

In Finnish mythology the *Aarnivalkea* are spots where an eternal flame associated with will-o'-the-wisp burns. They are claimed to mark the places where faerie gold is buried. They are protected by a glamour, or shapeshifting, that would prevent anyone finding them purely by chance.

Interestingly, in the New World, Mexico has two equivalents to these treasure lights as well. In one of these legends, these lights are associated with witches and are called *brujas*. Folklore explains the phenomenon to be witches who transformed into these lights. The reason for this, however, varies according to the region. Another explanation refers to the lights as indicators to places where gold or hidden treasures are buried, and which can be found only with the help of children. In this version, the earth lights are called *luces del dinero*, or money lights, or *luces del tesoro*, which translates as treasure lights.

Besides being the harbinger of treasure, more sinister tales of the will-o'-the-wisp can be found in numerous folk tales around the United Kingdom and is often a malicious character in the stories. In Welsh folklore, it is said that the light is faerie fire held in the hand of a *púca*, a small goblin-like faerie that mischievously leads lone travelers off the beaten path at night for devious purposes. As the traveler follows the *púca* through the marsh or bog, the fire is extinguished, leaving them lost. The *púca* is said to be one of the *Tylwyth Teg*, or a member of a faerie family. In Wales, the light predicts a funeral that will take place soon in the locality. The author, Wirt Sikes, in his book entitled *British Goblins* mentions the following Welsh tale about the *púca*:

A peasant travelling home at dusk sees a bright light moving along ahead of him. Looking closer, he sees that the light is a lantern held by a "dusky little figure," which he follows for several miles. Suddenly, he finds himself standing on the edge of a vast chasm with a roaring torrent of water rushing below him. At that precise moment the lantern-carrier leaps across the gap, lifts the light high over its head, lets out a malicious laugh and blows out the light, leaving the poor peasant a long way from home, standing in pitch darkness at the edge of a precipice. This is a fairly common cautionary tale concerning the phenomenon; however, the *ignis fatuus* was not always considered dangerous. Other stories tell of travelers getting lost in the woodland and coming upon a will-o'-the-wisp, and depending on how they treated the will-o'-the-wisp, the spirit would either get them lost further in the woods or guide them out.

These earth lights are so associated with faeries that they are even referred to as faerie lights. The Pixy-Light from Devon and Cornwall is most often associated with the Pixie who often has "pixie-led" travelers away from the safe and reliable route and into the bogs with glowing lights. Curiously, these lights can produce sounds, some even reproducing speech! Very interesting, indeed. In Cornish folklore, the Pixy-Light also has associations with the colt pixie. A colt pixie is a pixie that has taken the shape of a horse and enjoys playing tricks such as neighing at the other horses to lead them astray. There are also the reports of German faeries frequently blowing out candles on unsuspecting courting couples or producing obscene kissing sounds. The Pixy-Light was also associated with lambent light, literally tongues of flame, which the Old Norse had witnessed around their tombs. The folklore soon developed that these lights were guarding the tombs. My assumption is that certain peoples of these areas regarded the earth lights as denoting sacred places and that is the reason the dead were interred in these locations.

The will-o'-the-wisp was known as the spunkie in the Scottish Highlands where it would take the form of a linkboy which was a boy who carried a flaming torch to light the way for pedestrians in exchange for a fee. It was also said to simply be a light that always seemed to recede to lead unwary travelers to their doom. The spunkie has also been blamed for shipwrecks at night after being spotted on land and mistaken for a harbor light. Other tales of Scottish folklore regard these mysterious lights as omens of death or the ghosts of once living human beings. They often appeared over lochs or on roads along which funeral processions were known to travel. A strange light sometimes seen in the Hebrides is referred to as the *teine sith*, or "fairy light."

But aren't faeries silly things, you may be asking yourself. Faeries have always been seen, up until the Victorian period, as elementals. Faeries were the intelligences within the natural world. Even the author of the great detective, Sherlock Holmes, Sir Arthur Conan Doyle himself, believed in faeries and claimed that these elementals worked in unison with nature. The faeries were the transfer system between the sun and vegetation, one of the reasons why faeries are so associated with gardens. Doyle also believed that faeries did not have physical wings but what was seen as wings was the energetic aura around their bodies, a glowing emanation of energy that allowed for their transcendence through the various elements of the natural world. It is as if the body, the very physical essence of the faerie, was a biological rod to control what has come to be known as St. Elmo's fire. St. Elmo's fire, besides being a 1980s movie to spotlight the Brat Pack, is also a weather phenomenon in which luminous plasma is created by a corona discharge in an atmospheric electric field. The intensity of the effect, a blue or violet glow around an object, often accompanied by a hissing or buzzing sound, is proportional to the strength of the electric field and therefore noticeable primarily during thunderstorms or volcanic eruptions. My question is this: could St. Elmo's fire be an entity rather than a mere atmospheric discharge? William Shakespeare thought so. In Shakespeare's *The Tempest,* written in 1611, in Act I, Scene II, St. Elmo's fire acquires a more negative association, appearing as evidence of the tempest inflicted by Ariel according to the command of Prospero:

> PROSPERO
> Hast thou, spirit,
> Perform'd to point the tempest that I bade thee?
>
> ARIEL
> To every article.
> I boarded the king's ship; now on the beak,
> Now in the waist, the deck, in every cabin,
> I flamed amazement: sometime I'd divide,
> And burn in many places; on the topmast,
> The yards and bowsprit, would I flame distinctly,
> Then meet and join.
>
> — Act I, Scene II, *The Tempest*

The faerie's name, Ariel, even conjures the notion of electricity within the air, a natural intelligence that interacts with mankind who can only marvel at its power.

These intelligent fires are also mentioned as "death fires" in Samuel Taylor Coleridge's *The Rime of the Ancient Mariner*:

> About, about, in reel and rout,
> The death fires danced at night;
> The water, like a witch's oils,
> Burnt green and blue and white.

— l. 127–130

Like a banshee, these fires pronounced an imminent death, but they also behaved with intelligence.

Before we leave this realm of the fey, we must necessarily comment on the subject of portals which are a common theme in faerie lore and becoming a quite popular explanation in the paranormal world. One can be "taken" by a faerie by entering their world. Eating their food or even making physical contact can whisk you away from this world and sweep you into their realm. Faerie rings, often in the form of a circular formation of mushrooms, are also portals to their dimension.

What exactly is their dimension? The dimension of the elements, the non-physicality of the physical? Is their realm the Dreamtime conceived by the Australian Aboriginal people? As we have seen, these lights often lead people astray and they are never seen again. Where do they go? The space between spaces? Do they assimilate into the fabric of reality? These are questions that simply have no answer, but we can at least speculate.

As you can see, these earth lights are seen across time and space by various cultures. However, these lights abide by certain rules and are believed to be entities rather than just naturally occurring lights. They are not part of the same collective of natural processes such as wind and lightening but represent something wholly different yet still part of the natural world. However, as we shall see, some view these earth lights as visitations from sources outside of our own world.

Extraterrestrial Origins?

About 23 years ago I was on a bigfoot investigation in north central Pennsylvania. The area had a few reports of some strange activity such as locals near the forest reporting something large, walking on two legs, and going through their garbage. It was a pleasant summer evening, and two other investigators went out with me.

We were in an area that was second growth forest with pockets of mature hardwoods and palisades of evergreens. This location also had a wide swath cut through it to accommodate powerlines. These cleared areas are very good spots for catching glimpses of bear and coyote as they tend to live on the periphery of civilization. But, alas, this night there was nothing moving about. This area was fairly familiar to us as we have researched this land maybe a handful of times previously. We usually would encounter a large number of white-tailed deer or the occasional fox. But this night all was quiet and startlingly empty of any wildlife. Not even the plaintive howl of the coyote rattled through the darkness. We seemed to be alone.

Then a very pungent smell permeated the air to the point our eyes watered. We have scared up quite a few skunks in our wanderings and this smell was unlike anything we had faced before. It smelled like the sickening smell of rotted flesh, that undeniable smell of death one often encounters in the woods that usually leads to a deer that was hit by a car on the road a few miles away and managed to limp into the woods, hiding, only to succumb to its injuries and die. But this was very different. The smell was "ejected" into the night. It was directed at us the way a skunk would spray, focused squarely on us, but oddly this time there was no discernable source. We were in a clearing at this point, in the opening of the powerline corridor. What is even more unnerving, the smell changed, transitioning from the immediate smell of decomposition to one of urine and what smelled revoltingly similar to body odor. For some reason, that was the most frightening because it had such a human aspect to it. There was one more scent transition and that was to a very loamy scent of turned over earth, the smell of rich black soil. Then, as if someone had turned off the source, it immediately was gone with no notes of the smells even lingering in the still night air. We stood, alone, in the open, the constellations overhead, talking amongst ourselves about the origination of the smell.

I scoured the night, my eyes trying to peer deeper into the darkness, but the woods were thick and there was no ambient light. The moon had yet to breach the horizon, so we stood in a world of stark blackness. But something caught my eye on the cleared ridge above us, maybe a quarter mile from where we stood. A red light was moving across the horizon of the ridge. It was solid red. It did not flash, it simply moved silently in the night. But it did seem quite large. If you hold out your hand at arm's length and put up your thumb, the light we saw was about the size of the fingernail of the thumb. It moved very slowly and in a straight line. It had to be a plane, there was no other explanation. That is, until my fellow researcher, Jim, let out an audible gasp. We watched the light move across the clearing in the woods, but when it reached the embankment of trees on the other side, the light was in front of the trees! It wasn't far off, but this light was a bright red orb that was now moving within the trees themselves. It appeared as if this supposed plane had crashed in the forest, but no, it was undulating through the trees. It never came any closer to us. It made its way through the trees and disappeared. I can only assume that it kept its course and continued through the woods to who knows where.

I have never been much into the research of unidentified flying objects, but in any paranormal research, you will undoubtedly encounter them in some way, if only through a witnesses' testimony. But are these objects alien crafts? Something about this anomalous light blurs the perceived notions of supposedly established paradigms within the paranormal world. Many ardent researchers only focus on the cryptid aspect. They fall into different camps of belief, such as the flesh and blood camp, the camp that believes bigfoot and the like are alien visitations, and those who believe that this cryptid creature is interdimensional. Many aspects of a sighting are neglected or summarily disregarded because it doesn't make any sense to the researcher. In his or her mind the schema established in their belief is the framework for their quarry. If something is incongruent with their preconceived notions it is discarded or, more disparagingly, taken as a lie. I did interview one group of ghost hunters who kept an open mind, or this next story would not exist.

Several years ago, I sat down with a ghost hunting group who contacted me because they had an experience that simply did not make sense to them. They were investigating a dilapidated farmhouse in the middle of nowhere that was rumored to be haunted because—get this—brilliant orbs had been seen on the abandoned property and even seen moving within the house through the yellowing windows. This group got permission from the owners of the property to enter the house and conduct a night investigation. A few hours into the hunt, they were not disappointed. They began to see orbs and even have curious spikes on their EMF detector, a device used to measure electrical current in the environment. The house had no electricity running to it, so the spikes were exciting for the group. As often happens, this group encountered battery drain of their equipment. Not only the EMF detectors, but cameras and voice recorders were all experiencing an unusual draining of power.

One of the researchers who was elected to be the "tech guy" dutifully went to his car to gather equipment and recharge batteries. The night air was cold on his skin, even though it was August, but the farmhouse was muggy and stiflingly hot, and he enjoyed the respite in the night. The air was fresh, unlike the stale air he had been inhaling for the last two hours, filled with the unmistakable hints of mildew and mold. He opened the hatch to his SUV when his walkie talkie sputtered to chaotic life. "Do you see it?" A voice broke the static, then a female voice attempted to talk over that voice. Something was going on inside the house. The tech guy stepped away from his vehicle to listen intently on the conversation attempting to take place over the walkie talkie. What he could gather from the muffled excitement and the flurry of interruptions was that an orb of light was making its way through various areas of the farmhouse, floating from room to room, sometimes blinking out before reappearing to manifest in another room.

The tech guy, excited to return to the action, scrambled for batteries inside his trunk before hurriedly closing the hatch. But when he did, he noticed an odd reflection in the glass. Slowly turning, he looked up about twenty feet or so and there hovering silently in the night sky was a red orb. Then in an instant it went out. He related to me that he felt as if this thing wanted to be seen, as if there was some sort of imperative to its manifestation. Indeed, it seems as if there was. For when the hovering orb outside the farmhouse faded, so too did the orb inside the house. The instant the floating orb outside went out, the walkie talkie was filled with the voices of the people within the farmhouse announcing that the orb vanished.

The tech guy waited a few minutes on a hunch. Suddenly the orb in the air illuminated once more, still floating in the same position. Then the chorus of voices within the house began, giddy that the orb within the house could be seen. This went on for roughly ten minutes or so. The observer outside saw this hovering orb light itself then extinguish. As this was happening, the orb within the farmhouse was doing the same thing. Was this a ghostly manifestation? A UFO visitation? Both? Or something very different? Let's proceed, shall we?

The swampy area of Massachusetts known as the Bridgewater Triangle has a plethora of folklore concerning ghostly orbs of light, and there have been modern observations of these lights seen connected to the earth as well as reported UFOs within the skies over this area. But is there an historical precedent or is this a modern observation? In fact, the history of floating or flying orbs goes back millennia!

A Chinese polymath, Sheng Gua, may have recorded such a phenomenon in the *Book of Dreams*, stating,

> "In the middle of the reign of emperor Jia You, at Yanzhou, in the Jiangsu province, an enormous pearl was seen especially in gloomy weather. At first it appeared in the marsh... and disappeared finally in the Xinkai Lake."

It was described as very bright, illuminating the surrounding countryside and was a reliable phenomenon over ten years. This event occurred 1000 years ago! But there are far older accounts.

One of the first written accounts of flying orbs is the following excerpt from an Egyptian papyrus - part of the annals of Thutmose III, who reigned around 1504-1450 B.C.:

> In the year 22, of the 3rd month of winter, sixth hour of the day... the scribes of the House of Life found it was a circle of fire that was coming in the sky.... It had no head, the breath of its mouth had a foul odor. Its body one rod long and one rod wide. It had no voice. Their hearts became confused through it; then they laid themselves on their bellies....They went to the Pharaoh... to report it. His Majesty ordered .... [an examination of] all which is written in the papyrus rolls of the House of Life. His Majesty was meditating upon what happened. Now after some days had passed, these things became more numerous in the sky than ever. They shone more in the sky than the brightness of the sun, and extended to the limits of the four supports of the heavens.... Powerful was the position of the fire circles. The army of

the Pharaoh looked on with him in their midst. It was after supper. Thereupon, these fire circles ascended higher in the sky towards the south... The Pharaoh caused incense to be brought to make peace on the hearth... And what happened was ordered by the Pharaoh to be written in the annals of the House of Life... so that it be remembered for ever.

Again, we see this notion of fire related to these orbs. It isn't so much as we are talking about ancient people witnessing electric lights and attempting to comprehend what they are but more along the way of seeing what appeared to be living fire and trying to understand its meaning.

The Roman author Julius Obsequens, believed to have lived in the fourth century AD, drew on Livy as well as other sources of his time to compile his book *Prodigorium liber*, which describes many peculiar phenomena, some of which could be interpreted as flying orbs. Here are just a few examples:

216 B.C. Things like ships were seen in the sky over Italy... At Arpi (180 Roman miles, east of Rome, in Apulia) a round shield was seen in the sky. At Capua, the sky was all on fire, and one saw figures like ships...

99 B.C. When C. Murius and L. Valerius were consuls, in Tarquinia, there fell in different places.... a thing like a flaming torch, and it came suddenly from the sky. Towards sunset, a round object like a globe, or round or circular shield took its path in the sky, from west to east.

90 B.C. In the territory of Spoletium (65 Roman miles north of Rome, in Umbria) a globe of fire, of golden color, fell to the earth, gyrating. It then seemed to increase in size, rose from the earth, and ascended into the sky, where it obscured the disc of the sun, with its brilliance. It revolved towards the eastern quadrant of the sky.

A later chronicler of inexplicable phenomena, Conrad Wolffhart, a professor of grammar and dialectics who under the pen name of Lycosthenes wrote the compendium *Prodigiorum ac Ostentorum Chronicon*, published in 1567, mentions the following events:

> 393 A.D. Strange lights were seen in the sky in the days of the Emperor Theodosius. On a sudden, a bright globe appeared at midnight. It shone brilliantly near the day star [the planet Venis], about the circle of the Zodiac. This globe shone little less brilliantly than the planet, and little by little, a great number of other glowing orbs drew near the first globe. The spectacle was like a swarm of bees flying around the bee-keeper, and the light of these orbs was as if they were dashing violently against each other. Soon, they blended together into one awful flame, and bodied forth to the eye as a horrible two-edged sword. The strange globe which was first seen now appeared like the pommel to a handle, and all the little orbs, fused with the first, shone as brilliantly as the first globe.

A rare typeset book from 1493, now preserved in a museum at Verdun, France, contains what may be the earliest pictorial representation of a UFO in Europe. Hartmann Schedel, author of the book *Liber Chronicarum*, describes a strange fiery sphere witnessed in 1034, soaring through the sky in a straight course from south to east and then veering toward the setting sun. The illustration accompanying the account shows a cigar-shaped form haloed by flames, sailing through a blue sky over a green, rolling countryside.

Some people fixate on the arrow-shaped object that is sometimes referred to as a "craft." I, however, think we should focus on all the orbs in this picture! The orbs even seem to interact with the sun, as if two elements were intermingling. Notice, also, the fire burning within this illustration. Does the fire on the ground represent where these orbs emerged?

A term equivalent to our "flying saucer" was actually used by the Japanese approximately 700 years before it came into use in the West. Ancient documents describe an unusual shining object seen the night of October 27, 1180, as a flying "earthenware vessel." Remember flying saucers are so named because they resemble a saucer. Does anyone even use saucers nowadays? Whatever, back to the sighting. After a while the object, which had been heading northeast from a mountain in Kii province, changed its direction and vanished below the horizon, leaving a luminous trail. (Jacques Vallee, *Passport to Magonia*, p. 4-5)

Now we will jump continents and take a look at an English account. Here is a classical description from William of Newburgh's Chronicle of a flying saucer seen in England toward the end of the 12th century:

At Byland or Begland Abbey [the largest Cistercian abbey in England], in the North Yorkshire Riding, while the abbot and monks were in the refectorium, a flat, round, shining silvery object ["discus" is the word used in the Latin account] flew over the abbey and caused the utmost terror.

This must be an extraterrestrial visitation, correct? There is no other logical explanation, is there? Well let's look into what might be called the first official investigation of a UFO sighting.

This event occurred in Japan in 1235, during the night of September 24. While General Yoritsume and his army were encamped, there were observed mysterious lights in the heavens. The lights were seen in the southwest for many hours, winging, circling, and moving in loops. The general ordered a "full-scale scientific investigation" of these strange events. The report finally submitted to him by the investigators read: "the whole thing is completely natural, General. It is... only the wind making the stars sway."

Now you may scoff at such a conclusion, but this account stresses that it was a *natural* phenomenon. This was not alien, but very terrestrial. Again, my conclusion is that reports that occurred throughout history are viewed through a modern lens and technology is ascribed to the lights until they transform into "craft" rather than considering these lights as naturally occurring earth lights.

The European record of luminescent orbs continued throughout the 14th and 15th centuries:

1322 A.D. In the first hour of the night of Novr. 4... there was seen in the sky over Uxbridge, England, a pile [pillar] of fire the size of a small boat, pallid and livid in colour. It rose from the south, crossed the sky with a slow and grave motion, and went north. Out of the front of the pile, a fervent red flame burst forth with great beams of light. Its speed increased, and it flew thro' the air....

58

If we read closely, these flames were said to rise? Could that mean they rose out of the ground? Again, the elements described are natural.

> 1387 A.D. In Novr. and Decr. of this year, a fire in the sky, like a burning and revolving wheel, or round barrel of flame, emitting fire from above, and others in the shape of a long fiery beam, were seen through a great deal of the winter, in the county of Leicester, Eng., and in Northamptonshire.

It is very interesting that these accounts of strange lights occur in the fall or winter. In my experiences, this was a common thread in most of my cases as well.

These reports were all documented in the Middle Ages. As an historian, we must keep in mind the Medieval period was the age of faith. The Word of God informed every aspect of life. It may be from the Word of God that these sightings were shaped in the Medieval imagination.

One of the most famous and perhaps the most involving interaction with what I deem as earth lights is captured quite poetically in the Old Testament report by the prophet named Ezekiel:

> 4-9 I looked: I saw an immense dust storm come from the north, an immense cloud with lightning flashing from it, a huge ball of fire glowing like bronze. Within the fire were what looked like four creatures vibrant with life. Each had the form of a human being, but each also had four faces and four wings. Their legs were as sturdy and straight as columns, but their feet were hoofed like those of a calf and sparkled from the fire like burnished bronze. On all four sides under their wings they had human hands. All four had both faces and wings, with the wings touching one another.

They turned neither one way nor the other; they went straight forward.

The lights came out of the natural environment. There are also four beings seen. These are the personification of the elements. The prophet is experiencing Earth, air, fire, and water, revealed before him. They are seen as an assimilation of humans and animals, the union of mankind with nature.

10-12 Their faces looked like this: In front a human face, on the right side the face of a lion, on the left the face of an ox, and in back the face of an eagle. So much for the faces. The wings were spread out with the tips of one pair touching the creature on either side; the other pair of wings covered its body. Each creature went straight ahead. Wherever the spirit went, they went. They didn't turn as they went.

The wings represent the notion of transcendence, that these element beings can occupy all facets of Nature. And we see this same communion with the spirit, with the animating divinity within all the world. This is a Judaic setting emersed in animistic symbolism.

13-14 The four creatures looked like a blazing fire, or like fiery torches. Tongues of fire shot back and forth between the creatures, and out of the fire, bolts of lightning. The creatures flashed back and forth like strikes of lightning.

Tongues of flame, the lapping movement of an element which makes it appear alive, is highlighted in this passage. Take note that this flame is mired in the forces of Nature.

15-16 As I watched the four creatures, I saw something that looked like a wheel on the ground beside each of the four-faced creatures. This is what the wheels looked like: They were identical wheels, sparkling like diamonds in the sun. It looked like they were wheels within wheels, like a gyroscope.

This is the point where all the Ancient Astronaut theorists come out to pontificate. The wheel is chthonic, a Greek word meaning "of the earth." It comes out of our world, just like the earth lights.

17-21 They went in any one of the four directions they faced, but straight, not veering off. The rims were immense, circled with eyes. When the living creatures went, the wheels went; when the living creatures lifted off, the wheels lifted off. Wherever the spirit went, they went, the wheels sticking right with them, for the spirit of the living creatures was in the wheels. When the creatures went, the wheels went; when the creatures stopped, the wheels stopped; when the creatures lifted off, the wheels lifted off, because the spirit of the living creatures was in the wheels.

Again, we see these creatures residing in the elements. And the wheel is controlled by these elementals.

22-24 Over the heads of the living creatures was something like a dome, shimmering like a sky full of cut glass, vaulted over their heads. Under the dome one set of wings was extended toward the others, with another set of wings covering their bodies. When they moved I heard their wings—it was like the roar of a great waterfall, like the voice of The Strong God, like the noise of a battlefield. When they stopped, they folded their wings.

This passage is very interesting in that what is above is also below. That Heaven is somehow revealed within this scene. The shimmering cut glass visually would be sparkling lights in the sky.

61

25-28 And then, as they stood with folded wings, there was a voice from above the dome over their heads. Above the dome there was something that looked like a throne, sky-blue like a sapphire, with a humanlike figure towering above the throne. From what I could see, from the waist up he looked like burnished bronze and from the waist down like a blazing fire. Brightness everywhere! The way a rainbow springs out of the sky on a rainy day—that's what it was like. It turned out to be the Glory of God!

As above so below—God Himself is revealed in Nature itself. This is a monotheistic God, but all of nature acts in accordance with Divine will. God is in the natural world. This passage can literally be deconstructed as a shift from animism to the burgeoning doctrine that will become Judaism. All of nature is alive, yes, but God is in control. The lights seen in Nature is the revelation of the miraculous in our world.

This Old Testament encounter emanated out of the natural world. It involved light and fire and disembodied voices, something inherent in many incidents involving these orbs. Immediately, we, with our 21st century technical minds project our world onto the worldview of the ancients. This is a huge mistake, and it places the account out of context. This was the experience of a prophet in the desert when suddenly lights began to manifest and voices were heard. He relates witnessing living fire and sentient colors. There may be a neurological precedent implicated in many of these encounters as well. The direct effects of light are in synaptic circuits within our brain that directly impact our centers related to sleep, mood, and cognition. The indirect pathways affect the circadian clock first, which has vast connections to all physiological functions. These two complex systems interact in many ways that are not fully understood. One of these ways in which light may affect the brain is by producing hallucinations. Did this Old Testament prophet see beings or did the lights he witnessed trigger areas in his brain that induced him into perceiving forms? If he did indeed see these forms, are they related to the Wandjina of the Australian Aboriginal concept of the Dreamtime or to the Paracelsus worldview in which alchemy maintained that the natural world was imbued with intelligent elementals? Again, we have no definitive answer, but I want to make this book as interactive as possible and I ask you, the reader, to speculate as well.

Interestingly, the author Whitley Streiber, who documented his encounter with what he believed to be aliens in his book entitled *Communion* also described brilliant multicolored lights in a desolate area, in this case, the woods. It seems that many reports of what are labeled extraterrestrial are done so by our current beliefs. To me however, let us examine the reports *in situ*. There are lights seen in the desert or in the woods; they emanate from the wild places. They involve color and fire and voices. Occasionally we are told of beings associated with these lights. Again, can I at least suggest that the colors and lights had either a hallucinatory effect on the brain or can I conjecture that if these entities were indeed physically seen could they be the elementals within the natural world that have been witnessed by shamans for 200,000 years? Are these encounters involving beings of this world? I believe so. Let us examine the next case which may sharpen our focus a bit more.

During the era of Stuart Scotland, at the dawning of the age of Enlightenment, a certain pastor claimed to have visited the world of the faerie. The Reverend Robert Kirk, minister of the Parish of Aberfoyle, Stirling, Scotland, writing between 1688 and 1692, compiled a treatise on the fairy folklore of Scotland in the book *The Secret Lives of Elves and Fairies.* Kirk believed that he interacted with this Goblin Realm, and, in the end, left this plane of existence entirely and entered their universe wholly. He leaves us with an interesting description of this entryway opening up into this other realm:

"It was a fair evening in the month of May...A full round moon being lately risen...Then it was suddenly I heard a strange sound...I saw light, bright as day, issuing from [a mound]...There was no earthen door but... a shapely carven doorframe."

Kirk describes the sensation of being pulled into the doorway. Upon entering, Kirk states "the place smelled of roses or other flowers that blossom in the summer."

Reverend Kirk goes on to describe a passageway that leads to various rooms. He maintained "the very walls of the place gave forth light." Soon enough he encounters the inhabitants of the "mound." He saw "tall and stately beings...greater in height than any living man or woman, and very bright." Among these larger figures were "smaller, darker, stranger beings." This is not the world of science. Although aspects of the Enlightenment were taking some of the mystery out of the cosmos, the universe was still a very magical place. This has a very close parallel to UFO abduction stories, does it not? A person enters an object from another realm and is taken away? But this was not something unearthly; indeed, it was the earthliest experience one could have!

Reverend Kirk was a former resident of the Old Manse which is situated nearby on what is known as the Fairy Knowe. The same house is where Sir Walter Scott wrote his famous poem "The Lady of the Lake," also about a faerie. It was in these surroundings that Kirk interacted with the hidden world of the wee folk. Thanks to Kirk, we have insight into this world.

In *The Secret Commonwealth of Elves, Fauns and Fairies,* Kirk wrote:

"These Siths or Fairies they call Sleagh Maith or the Good People...are said to be of middle nature between Man and Angel, as were Daemons thought to be of old; of intelligent fluidous Spirits, and light changeable bodies (lyke those called Astral) somewhat of the nature of a condensed cloud, and best seen in twilight. These bodies be so pliable through the subtlety of Spirits that agitate them, that they can make them appear or disappear at pleasure."

This description is quite reminiscent of how Paracelsus described these ethereal elementals and Shakespeare's Ariel is recognizable in this description as well—and this coming from a pastor!

There is a reason I did not include this passage in the chapter regarding faeries. It is to illustrate how fluid and ambiguous the paranormal world really is and when studying a particular sighting, many other elements come into play. There is no black and white, no cut and dry in the paranormal world. There is and always will be the variables. Constants simply don't apply to metaphysics.

Before we wrap things up in this chapter, modern eyewitnesses have commented on what appears to be an extraterrestrial connection. Oddly, these accounts often involve a cryptid, such as a Bigfoot. For those who want to read further into this relationship I recommend Stan Gordon's authoritative account in his book *Silent Invasion*. He goes into great detail and investigates a majority of these sightings and encounters. I will need to recount and rehash one of these strange incidents, however, to examine some sort of connection between glowing orbs and Bigfoot and what is deemed to be a UFO and come to some conclusion to satisfy my inquiry on the subject.

This is a strange tale reported back in October of 1973. It happened in Fayette County, on a farm in a wooded area and was witnessed by fifteen people. A large red object was seen hovering low in the sky. After a while, the object apparently began emitting a mechanical droning noise and appeared to the witnesses to land in a field. Now that is strange in and of itself, but now, along with the whirling sound, came the high-pitched wails of what sounded like a crying baby. Some of those witnesses decided they must investigate this situation further, so they drove off in search of the spot the object landed.

Nearing the supposed site, the vehicle they drove had a sudden battery drain. Mustering a bravery that I cannot comprehend, they got out of the car and went into the field where they saw the object. It was no longer red but appeared to them as a glowing white dome that had an odd rubber smell associated with it. Now, if the sight of a brightly lit dome in the middle of a rural field isn't enough, two bipedal creatures were now seen approaching the object. As Stan Gordon notes on the incident in his book *Silent Invasion,* the creatures "were covered from head to toe with brownish-gray hair, some of which was hanging from their bodies. The first of the two beasts was…over eight feet tall…the other creature…seven feet." And they were still making that crying sound! Oh yes, one more thing. The creatures had large glowing green eyes.

So, what happened next, you may ask yourself. Well, as any good country boy would do, the witnesses took a shot at them. I guess his flight or fight response compelled him to fight. At this moment of firing on the beasts, the glowing object in the field vanished. The creatures eventually moved off and disappeared into the woods. But this tale is not over yet. A state police trooper arrived on the scene after a witness called for help. In the field, where the object had been, a glowing ring was evidenced. So bright was the illumination from this ring that it was said one could read by it even in the darkness of the night.

This is indeed a bizarre story. But this tale does have antecedents in different times and in very different places. As a point of consideration, I will now change the focus from an extraterrestrial explanation to an ultraterrestial possibility. Could this sighting and many more like it be evidence not of alien interaction with our world but evidence of our world interacting with the Goblin Realm where elementals reside?

Abductions today, and UFOs in general, in a world made up of science and industry, have a more industrial approach. However, the abductions almost always take place out in the forest, away from civilization. Of course, there are exceptions to this, but isn't it strange in a world that is ravishing the last vestiges of what it means to be wild and the woods are ever dwindling from the landscape, that close encounters take place in rural areas? As if the events belonged there? As if this was the natural place for these "aliens" to reside?

But even accounts made today tend to have a natural element imbedded within as well if you research below the surface. Whitley Strieber, famous for his *Communion* book series dealing with his alleged alien abductions, commented on his abductors smelling like cinnamon and their imagined "spacecraft" smelling of soil and mildew. Even Strieber recognized a natural, elemental aspect of his encounters. Do we tend to project our worldview onto the canvas of alien abductions? How are we to not! We are inundated by media that does not only report on alien abductions but, detrimentally, informs us of what we are supposed to be witnessing. So, too, does the motion picture industry. Since the 1953 film *Invaders from Mars* or *The Outer Limits* first aired on television in 1963, we know that aliens have bulbous heads and large, unblinking almond shaped eyes. They look like characters wearing masks because in essence they are characters wearing masks, the very images from the media saturation in which we were first exposed to them. If we had no exposure to the conception of alien appearance through the networks of entertainment, I wonder if the witnesses would report something far different. I believe they would indeed see their alien experience as something completely different.

This leads me inevitably to the question—are the UFOs seen around the world manifestations of earth lights? That would be a reason why strange luminescent anomalies seemingly appear and disappear so quickly. Is it possible that the lights seen in the sky are simply energy—akin to orbs witnessed by ghost investigators—and this energy is the visual evidence of the movement between dimensions? I have recorded reports taken from witnesses and observed the manifestations of unexplained lights myself, and I am coming to this conclusion.

The idea of a Goblin Universe is a reference to a parallel universe; this is a hypothetical self-contained separate reality co-existing with our reality. A specific group of parallel universes is called a "multiverse;" although, this term can also be used to describe the possible parallel universes that constitute reality and may converge in our area. This is supported by quantum-mechanics, something about which I have not a clue but let's just say it is a theory Carl Sagan wouldn't rule out. Ultraterrestrials is the term used to describe the inhabitants of these universes. Ken Korczak, writing for the website *Unexplained Mysteries* (unexplained-mysteries.com), gives this description of Ultraterrestrials:

> "a species that has always been here, which evolved on earth along with homo sapiens...All we know of them are fleeting glimpses of light in the sky, occasional bizarre encounters between human beings and so-called aliens, and other unexplainable phenomenon."

This too is an interesting notion. The investigator John Keel, made famous by his analysis into the Mothman mystery, even subscribed to this theory. It takes away explaining the near impossibility of interstellar space travel. We can connect the dots across time and space regarding encounters with elementals.

Modern Accounts

Even today, earth lights are witnessed by individuals with no affinity toward the paranormal. They simply encounter strange luminescent spheres appearing on the landscape or report odd curtains of light. However, these sightings of earth lights may not be solely by happenstance. Indeed, there may be a geological attachment associated with this enigma. There are many locations in the United States where earth lights are seen, though they go by the names "ghost lights," "spook lights," or some regional name usually devised to lure in tourists to buy cheap souvenirs.

Here are but a few listings of the more famous sites for earth lights gathered from accounts around the world. Unfortunately, many of these tales involve ghosts because, in the realm of the paranormal, a haunting seems most logical. But please, as you read these various accounts from around the world, consider the metaphysical as a possible answer to this luminous quagmire.

United States

The Maco Station Light

The Maco Station Light is seen in North Carolina. The tale associated the light with the ghost of Joe Baldwin, a train conductor who was said to have been decapitated in a collision that occurred in Maco between a runaway passenger car in the late 1800s. The Maco Light is an anomalous "ghost light," occasionally seen between the late 19th century and 1977. The locals suggest the light is a lantern, carried by the ghost of John Baldwin, still searching for his missing head. The light was never formally explained but was often thought to be the result of marsh gas from nearby swamps or the refraction of lights from a highway. The light is said to appear in the distance, before approaching along the tracks facing East, rising to a height of about 5 feet, and either flying to the side of the track in an arc or receding from the witness. Other reports speak of green or red lights, or other patterns of movement by the orb.

The Brown Mountain Lights

The Brown Mountain Lights are seen in North Carolina and the only earth lights to have a country song dedicated to it. The earliest published references to strange lights there are from around 1910. One early account of the lights dates from September 24, 1913, as reported in the *Charlotte Daily Observer*. It described "mysterious lights seen just above the horizon every night," red in color, appearing "punctually" at 7:30 PM and again at 10 PM. These lights were even encountered and chased by the local police, the officers claiming the lights reached speeds in excess of 70 miles per hour! The Brown Mountain Lights are technically a spook light because many locals believe it is the ghost of someone from either the Revolutionary War or the Civil War. However, as UFOs gain in popularity, the notion of these being spook lights is losing traction and a more modern sensibility is transforming this light into proof of extraterrestrial visitations.

Hornet Spook Light

The Hornet Spook Light is seen in various regions around the state of Missouri. The Spook Light, also called the Hornet Spook Light, Hollis Light and Joplin Spook Light, is a ghost light reported to appear in a small area known locally as the "Devil's Promenade" on the border between southwestern Missouri and northeastern Oklahoma, west of the small town of Hornet, Missouri. The light has been seen in backyards of the area and has been spotted both near to and far away from sightseers. Its color is also inconsistent, with some eyewitnesses reporting a greenish glow, while others describe it as orange, red, yellow, or even blue.

It is almost always said to be in the shape of a ball, although some say it more closely resembles a camping lantern traveling a couple of feet off the ground. One piece of folklore concerning the nature of these lights is that they are the disembodied spirits of two American Indian lovers who still search for each other in the afterlife. The light is most commonly described as being visible from inside the Oklahoma border looking to the west. The Spook Light is usually described as a single ball of light or a tight grouping of lights that is said to appear in the area regularly, usually at night.

Marfa Lights

The Great State of Texas boasts the Marfa lights. Also known as the Marfa ghost lights, this anomaly has been observed near U.S. Route 67 on Mitchell Flat east of Marfa, Texas. They have gained some fame as onlookers have attributed them to paranormal phenomena such as ghosts, UFOs, or the will-o'-the-wisp. The first historical record of the Marfa lights was in 1883 when a young cowhand, Robert Reed Ellison, saw a flickering light while he was driving cattle through Paisano Pass and wondered if it was the campfire of Apache Indians. Other settlers told him they often saw the lights, but that when they investigated, they found no ashes or other evidence of a campsite. Joe and Anne Humphreys next reported seeing the lights in 1885. These enigmatic orbs are said to suddenly appear above desert foliage. These balls of light may remain stationary as they pulse on and off with intensity varying from dim to almost blinding brilliance. Other times, these ghostly lights may scurry across the desert or perform aerial divisions and mergers in which one light appears to be absorbed by the other. Light colors are usually yellow orange but other hues, including green, blue and red are also seen.

Hebron Light

Maryland has a phenomenon known as the Hebron Light. Sightings of the pinkish-orange ghost light had been recorded on and off for some 75 years along the rural Eastern Shore village. Longtime Hebron residents felt the appearance of the mysterious light was somehow connected to the hanging of a slave in the woods years earlier during the Civil War. Others suggested that the light is ectoplasm, the energy left over after a body departs this world. They hypothesize that it is the residue of the notorious Patty Cannon, an 18th-century slave trader and murderess who lured her victims, estimated at between 17 to 50, into a tavern she owned near the Mason-Dixon Line, and killed them with arsenic.

The Paulding Light

The light appears in a valley outside of Paulding, Michigan, in the Upper Peninsula, near Watersmeet off US 45 on Robbins Pond Road/Old US 45. Without any explanation, this light is also known as a ghost light. The first recorded sighting of the Paulding Light was in 1966 when a group of teenagers reported the light to a local sheriff. Since then, a number of other individuals have reported seeing the light, which is said to appear nearly every night at the site.

Although stories related to the light vary, the most popular legend involves the death of a railroad brakeman. The legend states that the valley once contained railroad tracks and the light is the lantern of the brakeman who was killed while attempting to prevent an oncoming train from colliding with railway cars stopped on the tracks. Another story claims the light is the ghost of a slain mail courier, while another fanciful legend says that it is the ghost of an American Indian dancing on the power lines that run through the valley.

Canada

The St. Louis Light

The St. Louis Light, St. Louis Ghost Light, or St. Louis Ghost Train is a paranormal phenomenon seen near Saint Louis,

Saskatchewan, Canada. It has been described by witnesses as a huge beam of white light, reminiscent of a headlight on an old-fashioned train. Because it looks like this, the folklore surrounding this light inevitably led to the luminescence being the ghost of someone killed on the tracks. A strange light moving up and down along an old, abandoned rail line at night, changing colors and varying in brightness has been reported. The rail line, located south of Prince Albert and north of St. Louis, has had its tracks removed, but the phenomenon still occurs on a regular basis.

Australia

The Min Min Lights

The Min Min lights are quite known in the Land Down Under, reported in the desolation that is the Australian Outback. Stories about the lights can be found in several Aboriginal Australian cultures predating the European colonization of Australia and have since become part of wider Australian folklore. These Min Min lights are often portrayed as benign, yet frightening and unknowable to those who experience them. Accounts of the light appearances vary, though they are most commonly described as being fuzzy, disc-shaped lights that appear to hover just above the horizon. They are often described as being white, though some accounts describe them as changing color from white to red to green and back again. Some accounts describe them as being dim while others describe them as being bright enough to illuminate the ground under them and to cause nearby objects to cast clearly defined shadows. According to folklore, the lights sometimes follow or approach people and disappear when confronted, sometimes very rapidly, only to reappear later. It is also whispered that anyone who chases the lights and catches them will never return to tell the tale, a common attribute seen in tales of the will-o'-the-wisp.

Asia

Mekong Lights

"Naga fireballs" or "Mekong lights" and, formerly, "ghost lights," are a phenomenon said to be seen annually on the Mekong River in Southeast Asia. Glowing balls are alleged to naturally rise from the water high into the air. The balls are said to be reddish and to range in size from smaller sparkles up to the size of basketballs. They quickly rise to a couple of hundred meters before disappearing. The number of fireballs reported varies between dozens to thousands per night. The phenomenon is locally attributed to *phaya nak*, a giant serpent, called a naga in local vernacular, which is said to live in the Mekong.

Chir Batti

Chir Batti, Chhir Batti or Cheer batti is a ghost light reported in the Banni grasslands, a seasonal marshy wetlands and adjoining desert of the marshy salt flats of the Rann of Kutch near the India–Pakistan border in Kutch district, Gujarat, India. Local villagers refer to the light as Chir Batti in the Kutchhi-Sindhi language, with Chir meaning "ghost" and Batti meaning "light."

It is described as an unexplained light occurring on dark nights as bright as a mercury lamp that changes its color to blue, red and yellow and resembles a moving ball or, occasionally, a pear-shaped form of fire, which may move as fast as an arrow but may also suddenly stop. According to local folklore, these lights have been a part of life in the Banni grasslands and the adjoining Rann of Kutch for centuries but are little known beyond the immediate area. People continue to call them "ghost lights." Witnesses claim the lights to be sentient, at times even appearing to be playing hide and seek or following them. Some reports claim the light can only be seen after 8 pm on dark nights, are always two to ten feet above the ground, and if followed during the night, one could be misled from the road and lose their way in thorny jungles or desert of the salt flats of the Rann.

A team of local and US ornithologists and soldiers of the Indian Border Security Force who patrol the adjoining Rann of Kutch international border area of India with Pakistan have allegedly seen the light.

Europe

The Hessdalen Lights

The Hessdalen Lights are unidentified lights observed over a seven-and-a-half-mile stretch of the Hessdalen valley in rural central Norway. The Hessdalen Lights are of unknown origin. They appear both by day and by night and seem to float through and above the valley. They are usually bright white, yellow, or red and can appear above and below the horizon. The duration of the phenomenon may be a few seconds to well over an hour. Sometimes the lights move with enormous speed; at other times they seem to sway slowly back and forth. On yet other occasions, they hover in mid-air.

Unusual lights have been reported in the region since at least the 1930s. Especially high activity occurred between December 1981 and mid-1984, during which the lights were observed 15 to 20 times per week, attracting many overnight tourists. As of 2010, the number of observations had dwindled, with only 10 to 20 sightings yearly.

Granted, there are more locations on this globe that have reported earth lights, but the most interesting events are those that occur in a specific location over a long period of time, and these are a few locations worldwide that are still active today. There are an almost innumerable number of locations in total though. For example, there are several in just the relatively small land space of the British Isles. But the ones included in this chapter are the most enduring and iconic.

A Perfect Storm

I have been blessed to have done a fair amount of television and video documentaries about the paranormal. In fact, I have been a talking head, taking on the role of historian and cryptozoologist in various endeavors, and I have been employed as a writing contributor on several projects. In 2019, I joined the cast of *True Terror,* hosted by ol' Freddie Krueger himself, Robert Englund. I appeared on all six episodes of the series that ran on *Travel Channel.* Unfortunately, although the show did have merit, it debuted the same day as the international lockdown against the COVID virus and everyone was understandably tuned to news channels and the show was canceled quite quickly. I have appeared and contributed to part of three seasons of the Canadian program, *Red Earth Uncovered,* which looks at the paranormal from the angle of the indigenous peoples of our neighbor to the North. I am very proud of my work with that series and was honored to be asked to appear on their episodes. But it was the occasion to work with *Small Town Monsters* and the experiences I had filming segments of their program *Sasquatch Unearthed: The Ridge* that led me to write this book.

Seth Breedlove was filming two projects simultaneously and I was asked to appear in both. I have always admired Seth's approach to the unexplained and his stylized cinematography that his projects are known for. I first appeared in *American Werewolves,* in which I used history as a plow to uncover the fertile soil of werewolf folklore from the past. The other project being filmed was *Sasquatch Unearthed: The Ridge.* The ridge in the title refers to the Chestnut Ridge which runs from Morgantown, West Virginia and makes its way through several Western Pennsylvanian counties. It is on this ridge that I have conducted most of my research and where I first experienced the phenomenon of the earth lights. I even gained notoriety with the publication of my first book on the paranormal, entitled *The Unexplained World of the Chestnut Ridge.* Other local investigators and researchers, such as Bigfoot enthusiasts Eric Altman and Tom Mihok and the grandfather of paranormal research, Stan Gordon, were also part of this project. It was the first night at a location on the Chestnut Ridge in Fayette County that I joined the production team.

We were investigating an alleged highway sighting of a large hairy biped witnessed crossing a road. Very near that site, Eric Altman knew of an area that was rife with sightings, so that was the intended destination for the night's filming. It required 4-wheel drives with lift kits to carry us down a boulder strewn logging road. When we finally arrived, my kidneys feeling as if they went through several rounds with a prize fighter after all the jostling of the vehicle, I was startled how desolate the location was from, well, anything. The night was enveloped in a deep blackness and a heavy canopy of clouds suffocated any celestial light. It was still, warm, and isolated. For a filmed hunt for the elusive bigfoot, these were perfect circumstances. The mood was set, and filming began.

After Eric set up some sound collecting equipment, Heather Moser of the *Small Town Monsters* crew took a handful of researchers and a cameraman down a path through the woods that led to an old, abandoned miners cemetery. Seth and I would make our way several hundred yards up the road we came down. From that vantage point, the cemetery lay hidden by the trees, but it sat below us around half a mile away. Seth recorded me as I answered several of his questions concerning my thoughts on the nature of Bigfoot. The first couple hours were quiet with only a lone coyote piercing the stillness with its echoing cry that resounded off the hills of the hollows like a ricocheting bullet. Then Seth asked if I would do a couple of tree knocks.

Why do documenting crews so often resort to tree knocks? The answer is quite simple—it is action. Anything televised needs action to hold a viewer's attention, and tree knocks certainly break up the agonizing monotony of nothing happening. But guess what? Rarely does anything happen. That is why crews film for days and days to end up with 45 minutes of televised information. Paranormal entertainment is a slippery slope. I prefer to instruct rather than look for definitive evidence of a cryptid or a ghost, but I have been known to do some things purely for entertainment value. So, I proceeded to hit a tree three times with an ax handle. Why three times? Well, it's the woods and there are always sounds in the woods. Trees rub together, limbs fall, twigs snap. We are looking for a pattern. The idea is if something intelligent is in the woods they will respond in the same pattern, thus alerting us to the possibility that something is out there. Does it work? Rarely. But oddly, on this occasion, the wood knocks were answered by a howl that seemed in the disorienting darkness to emanate from the hill above where Seth and I stood.

Using the thermal imaging of the FLIR, nothing was revealed. Just the starkness of the trees. The howl may have been a coyote. It was certainly not a yelp, but it was short and inconclusive. But shortly following the howl, another sound faintly rose on the breeze that began to rustle the leaves. It was a faint "tink" sound, almost the same pitch and quality of windchimes. Oddly, as soon as I heard this sound, the other team who was down at the cemetery reported over the walkie talkie that they were hearing a tinking sound as well! They were asked if the graveyard had any decorations that could explain the sound and they replied that nothing down there could produce what we were hearing.

Then quite alarmingly Seth and I heard a crash to our right. Not a commotion in the woods, but the sound of a table collapsing or something heavy falling. It was where Eric and his son, Josh, were stationed and it sounded as if they'd dropped a lot of equipment. Well, so much for a clandestine investigation. With the night so harshly disturbed, Seth and I made our way back to Eric's position.

Now things were getting strange. Eric and Josh were set up and monitoring the location. They not only were not the ones responsible for the crashing and clamoring, but they also didn't even hear it! Seth and I explained that was impossible, that the origin of the commotion originated in and around their location and to our amazement they were unaware of any disturbance. And they did not hear the tinking sound either. They stood monitoring a silent wooded hollow with nothing to report.

By this time, it was getting late. From a production point of view, Seth did document intrepid researchers on the hunt for the elusive cryptid known as Bigfoot. And whatever it was, he did capture a howl of unknown origin. As most television shows go, Seth recorded about 95% more evidence than most! Throw in some interviews and he would have a solid hour of programming. To end the investigation, he and Eric made their way to the cemetery while Josh and I stayed back.

As Eric and Seth disappeared into the darkness, the sound of a windchime could be heard flitting throughout the hollow below. It wasn't multiple notes, mind you, but sounded as if one tube was struck and then another. There was a variation in pitches, but it wasn't a constant melody. Hey, I am not a music guy! That is how I can explain it. It still keeps me up at night. It was a tinking sound followed by another tinking sound that came from different locations. Think of it this way—as researchers, we employ wood knocks in the conjecture that something intelligent would respond in a pattern. In writing this now, just two months after the incident, I can now say quite lucidly that I feel as if we, the investigators, were getting "wood knocked." Except whatever was alerting us to its presence was not using sticks but a frequency. Look, I understand your incredulousness as a reader. If I were reading this right now, I would say, "Yeah, right." But what I am telling you is quite true and even now raises goosebumps as I am writing this at 10:27 am. I was writing last night at 11:30 pm but I stopped before I related this part because I wanted it to be light out. You see, after we heard these melodious tinks in the middle of the woods on a pitch-black night, the lights began to show themselves. Now I am getting the chills.

Josh and I saw the lights at the exact same time I believe. We weren't using a flashlight and without any ambient lighting our eyes were well adjusted to the darkness. We couldn't see deeply into the woods but our rods and cones were quite adapted to the environment so we could detect movement and illumination. Off to our right, we saw three lights emerge low to the ground. Because we had no landmarks to judge by, the lights seem to rise out of the bushes below, but I am not certain. Obviously, it was Seth and Eric and another investigator. The lights didn't look like flashlights but had the same quality as a cell phone screen or possibly a lantern with a single flame. Considering all the earth light locations in the United States I listed in the last chapter, I can see why so many involve the legends of a train. These lights were uncannily like a flame in an oil lamp. They swayed back and forth in a gentle motion as if the lights were being carried by someone walking. Oh, until they began to float. I can't leave that part out. It was then that Josh and I knew immediately that these lights had nothing to do with the production nor were they manmade.

As these lights appeared to be people walking, carrying something luminescent, they began to rise as if they were climbing an invisible staircase within the woods. They kept the same deliberate cadence and distance from one another then slowly began to rise until they had to be over twenty feet in the air and walking in the treetops. I immediately called out on the walkie talkie and explained what Josh and I were witnessing. The others could not see the lights in the trees, but they were more concerned with what was happening in front of them. There, in the graveyard in the hollow, was a light as well! They described hearing windchimes before it revealed itself! Josh and I could not see their light as it was too deep in the hollow, but the lights we could see in the trees, these yellow orbs, now began to separate within themselves and form two orbs from the one. They then appeared to fall from the height they had climbed, only to disappear in the woods below. That is when we heard over the walkie talkies that there were orbs everywhere among the trees down in the hollow!

Josh and I made our way quickly down the path that led to the graveyard. We could hear the confused and jumbled voices of our team shouting out and we could see orbs, some white, some yellow, some red, others green, moving through the trees. It made no logical sense. It appeared as if a group of people were playing tag with multicolored flashlights in the forest. There was a clearing where the cemetery lay; there weren't many headstones and the space was not large, probably the size of a large suburban backyard. But the lights seemed to stay out of the clearing and instead danced among the trees. As a writer, I thought about changing the verb "danced" a few times before committing to it. But there is no way else to explain it. These lights, these orbs, seemed to be playfully gamboling throughout the trees. I didn't feel fear, but I felt instinctually that these lights were biological, and they were sentient. They had to be. They were moving at times, stationary at others, and they seemed to be affecting everyone differently. Some of our team ran off into the woods pursuing them, diligently attempting to document these orbs, while others of our team just watched in frozen amazement and baffled bewilderment. These orbs also interacted with people personally.

I have been a friend of Tom Mihok's for a number of years. He is an intelligent man, the perfect researcher because he is an open-minded skeptic. But for whatever reason, the lights seemed to have homed in on him. They were coming close to him, and he followed them, leaving the group to explore out of his own curiosity. When he became isolated from us, an orange orb the size of a basketball left the wood line and entered the open path. It came out to meet Tom face to "face." Again, this is speculative commentary, but it makes sense. It just floated there, a ball of luminous energy. Tom said at one point it was only about five feet away. He reached out to touch it and it vanished! He quickly snapped on his flashlight and the beam fell onto the emptiness of trees. He was alone. Very soon all of the orbs disappeared. They simply vanished and the woods were quiet.

I asked Tom what did he think would have happened if he made physical contact with the light. He grew pale and his eyes widened. He said he had the feeling if he touched it he may never have been seen again.

Here is the synopsis of his sighting in his own words:

On March 16th, 2022, between the Chestnut & Laurel Ridges in Pennsylvania, I had a very close encounter with some Light anomalies. Different people will classify these anomalies as a variety of things. Mini Ufo's, Spirit energy (Spook Lights), Elemental Spirits, etc. I will begin my account by stating that I have no idea what these light anomalies were.

I was out with our research group, The Pennsylvania Bigfoot Society, investigating an area that has been very active recently. I was joined by several other members of the PBS including, Eric Altman, Ron Murphy, Connie, Chris, & Josh Brinker & Ricky Churby. This area is very remote and difficult to get to. It includes a clearing and cemetery that sits in the middle of a few mountain roads that are difficult to travel on, even in 4-wheel drive vehicles.

We broke up into 2 groups. Connie, Ricky, and myself were stationed at the clearing next to the cemetery, while Chris and Josh were with Eric set up about a mile down the road and around the bend in a pull off. The evening began with a strange howl and "whoop" call that was heard by several team members. Next, several team members heard a metallic "wind chime" sounds coming from the tree line. Connie & Ricky investigated the cemetery and trees to see if something explainable was causing the sound. They found nothing that could have caused the sounds we were hearing.

At this point, the entire group began seeing strange light anomalies. Eric and his group saw lights moving through the trees, Connie saw flashes of light in the tree line near the clearing, & I saw

2 small crystal blue colored lights just within the trees on the left side of the road that led to Eric's group.

It was at this point two lights appeared on the road between the two groups. One light was a white/orange color, about the size of a cantelope. The other light was a brilliant red color, about the size of a basketball. Both groups, from their own vantage points, witnessed the lights at the same time. I was amazed at how big and brilliantly defined the light spheres were, so I began to jog down the road towards the lights to get a closer look. To my surprise, the lights seemed to move towards me as I continued towards them. At this time, I slowed my pace to a walk, but kept moving. The only light on the road were the 2 light spheres us the flashlight I held in my hand had remained off since I started moving towards the lights.

At this point, I was now within 5 to 7 feet of the lights, both of us still slowly moving towards each other. There was no sound or odor of any kind. The lights did not leave a light trail as they moved. They just "floated" in the air slowly towards me. Thinking that maybe, I was approaching someone from the other group I began to ask "who is there", but, as soon as my voice became audible, both lights instantly disappeared. I immediately turned on my flashlight only to confirm that I was completely alone. I was standing on the dark road about half the distance from each group.
-Tom Mihok

Isn't it odd that Tom believed instinctually that if he touched the light he would not be seen from again? Does this incident not conjure the notion of the will-o'-the-wisp from ancient European folklore? Or the numerous accounts of these light anomalies from around the world which are rumored to lead travelers astray? Was what we witnessed the continuity of tales of these lights told from around the world?

Tom and I believe these lights were sentient energies. These bioluminescent entities are called by different names from around the world. If this light display occurred in a different setting near a sacred place this incident would be called a religious experience. At the very least we had a metaphysical encounter. Were we witness to the energy of the Earth? Did we have a revelation into the Divine tongues of flame that link the universe together into one sacred fire? Could these lights have been extraterrestrial probes? Did these lights denote the opening of a portal into another dimension? Were these the same lights seen in the Dreaming of the Australian aboriginals? In that culture we would have witnessed the Wandjina. If we were in Arabia, we would have encountered the jinn in this desolate area. I believe what we saw that night were elementals, the intelligences within the natural world.

Let me leave you with this note. Fayette County means "little fairy." Was this area so named because of these light anomalies? And did the name serve as a warning to all those foolish enough to enter the woods after dark?

A Final Word

I am thankful to have worked with excellent researchers and documentarians in my exploration of things considered paranormal and metaphysical. To them, I am greatly indebted. It is through these people that I have engaged in open dialog, and it is their enquiring minds that will allow us to cast a light into the preternatural darkness that engulfs so many supernatural subjects.

Thanks to Seth Breedlove, Heather Moser, and the entire team over at *Small Town Monsters* for not only their support but also for their exemplary documentation and elucidation into a wide range of subjects and for not laughing at my ideas concerning the fey and elementals. Also, thanks for making me look good through skilled editing. You make me look like I almost know what I am talking about! Without their invite into their crazy world of filmmaking, this book would never have seen the light of day!

Thanks to YOU folks as well for helping me connect the dots in this exploration of earth lights from around the world. We went down the rabbit hole together and are left now with more questions than when we began. I think any good course, regardless of the subject, should always leave the student open-eyed and curious about this world in which we live. There are no experts in the field of the paranormal and if there is one who self-reports as such, steer clear. I only know that what I wrote to you about concerning these earth lights is absolutely true.

If you would like to see video of some of the research we conducted in our investigation in Fayette County, please go to YouTube. Once there, go to *Small Town Monsters*. The evidence will be found under the program entitled *Sasquatch Unearthed: The Ridge,* episodes 1 and 2. There you will see the footage.

I urge you to examine the evidence and draw your own conclusions.

Bibliography

Allchin, Douglas, "Monsters & Marvels: How Do We Interpret the "Preternatural"?" *The American Biology Teacher*, November 2007.

Arrowsmith, Nancy. *Field Guide to the Little People: A Curious Journey into the Hidden Realm of Elves, Faeries, Hobgoblins, and Other Not-So-Mythical Creatures.* Llewellyn, 2009.

Ashlimans, D.L. *Changelings.* University of Pittsburgh.

Blavatsky, H.P. *The Key to Theosophy.* CreateSpace, 2017.

Briggs, Katherine. *An Encyclopedia of Fairies, Hobgoblins, Brownies, Bogies, and Other Supernatural Creatures.* Pantheon, 1978.

Brown, Donald. *Human Universals.* Philadelphia, Temple University Press, 1994.

Campbell, Joseph. *Primitive Mythology.* Penguin: New York, 1991.

Cavendish, Richard *The World of Ghosts and the Supernatural.* Waymark Publications, Basingstoke 1994.

Chaucer, Geoffrey. *The Canterbury Tales.* CreateSpace, 2018.

Cheung, Theresa. *The Element Encyclopedia of the Psychic World.* Harper Collins, 2009.

Coleman, Loren. *Cryptozoology A to Z.* Simon and Schuster 1999.

De Troyes, Chretien. *Arthurian Romances.* Penguin Classics, 2004.

Devereux, Paul. *Earth Lights.* Book Club Associates, 1984.

Drew, Samuel. *Cornwall.* 1824.

Eliade, Mircea. *The Sacred and the Profane: The Nature of Religion.* Harcourt Brace Jovanovich, 1987.

El-Zein, Amira. *Dictionary of Modern Written Arabic.* Spoken Language Services, 1993.

--*Medieval Islamic Civilization: An Encyclopedia.*

Felton, D. *Haunted Greece and Rome.* University of Texas, 2010.

Frazier, James. *The Golden Bough.* Oxford University Press: London 2009.

Froud, Brian and Lee, Alan. *Faeries.* Abrams, 2010.

Geoffrey of Monmouth. *Historia Regum Britanniae.*

Greenblatt, Stephen. *The Norton Shakespeare.* 3rd Ed. W.W. Norton and Company, 2015.

Godwin, William. *Lives of the Necromancers.* CreateSpace, 2015.

Guiley, Rosemary Ellen. *The Encyclopedia of Ghosts and Spirits.* Checkmark Books, 2007.
-- *The Djinn Connection: The Hidden Link Between Djinn, Shadow People, ETs, Nephilim, Archons, Reptilians and Other Entities.* Visionary Living, 2013.

Internetshakespeare.uvic.ca

Jolly, Clifford J. and Plogg, Fred. *Physical Anthropology and Archaeology.* 4th Ed. McGraw-Hill: New York, 1987.

Jung, Carl. *The Undiscovered Self: With Symbols and the Interpretation of Dreams.* Taylor and Francis Books, 2013.

Keightley, Thomas. *The Fairy Mythology.* 2016.

Kelly, Penny. "Nature Spirits—Their Intelligence and Form." *Fate,* March 2000.

King James. *Daemonologie.* CreateSpace, 2016.

Kirk, Robert. *The Secret Commonwealth of Elves, Fauns and Fairies.* Dover Publications 2008.

Map, Walter. *De nugis curialium Eyrbyggja.*

Meldrum, Jeff. *Sasquatch: Legend Meets Science.* Forge Books, 2007.

Olaus Magnus. *History of the Goths.* 1628.

Paracelsus. *Liber de Nymphis, sylphs, pygmaeis et salamandris et de caeteris spiritibus.*
-- *Philosophia Magna.*

Shuker, Karl. *The Unexplained.* World Pubns, 1996.

Spenser, Edmund. *The Faerie Quenne.* 2nd. Ed. Longman, 2006.

Unexplainedmysteries.com

Victorianweb.com

Wehr, Hans. *Medieval Islamic Civilization: An Encyclopedia.* Looh
    Press. 1994.

William of Newburgh. *Historia rerum Anglicarum.* BiblioLife, 2009.

Wordsworth, Jonathan. *The Penguin Book of Romantic Poetry.*
    Penguin, 2006.

Wright, Joseph. *The English Dialect Dictionary.* 1901.